END
ANXIETY!

END ANXIETY!

Proven Benefits of the
Transcendental Meditation Program

James G. Meade, PhD

SelectBooks, Inc.
New York

Author's Note

I am not a medical doctor, and teachers of the TM® program do not give advice on medical matters. I am a teacher of the TM® program and recommend the practice. This book is my own and does not speak officially for the Transcendental Meditation® program and the Transcendental Meditation® movement. This book has been written and published for educational purposes to enhance one's well-being. Information given herein is not intended to be a substitute for an individual's prescribed medications or psychological treatments or therapies. Reliance on any information provided herein is at your own risk. The publisher and author will have no responsibility to any person or entity with respect to loss, damage, or injury claimed to be caused directly or indirectly by any information in this book.

This edition published by SelectBooks, Inc.
For information address SelectBooks, Inc., New York, New York.

First Edition

ISBN 978-1-59079-523-1

Library of Congress Cataloging-in-Publication Data

Names: Meade, James G., author.
Title: End anxiety! : proven benefits of the Transcendental Meditation
    program / James G. Meade, Ph.D.
Description: First Edition. | New York, NY : SelectBooks, 2022. | Includes
    bibliographical references and index. | Summary: "Longtime instructor
    of the Transcendental Meditation® program shares stories about his
    firsthand experience of teaching the TM® technique to help hundreds of
    people turnaround their problems; he presents data from scientific
    studies to lay out evidence that practicing TM® is more effective for
    helping anxiety, depression, grief, and addiction than other forms of
    meditation and treatments—Provided by publisher."
Identifiers: LCCN 2022003618 (print) | LCCN 2022003619 (ebook) | ISBN
    9781590795231 (paperback) | ISBN 9781590795507 (ebook)
Subjects: LCSH: Anxiety. | Transcendental Meditation.
Classification: LCC BF575.A6 M424 2022 (print) | LCC BF575.A6 (ebook) |
    DDC 152.4/6--dc23/eng/20220603
LC record available at https://lccn.loc.gov/2022003618
LC ebook record available at https://lccn.loc.gov/2022003619

The illustrations printed in this book are adapted by the publisher with permission from the Maharishi Foundation USA. The Maharishi Foundation USA is the sole owner of all the original illustrations and retains all rights provided by copyright law.

Manufactured in the United States of America
10 9 8 7 6 5 4 3 2 1

In memory of my dear friend and mentor,
Marty Zucker, 1937–2020

CONTENTS

Foreword

I am amazed by the volume of scientific research—close to 700 studies and counting—that has been done on the Transcendental Meditation® program since my first paper was published by *Science* magazine in 1970. When Maharishi Mahesh Yogi, the founder of the Transcendental Meditation® program, came to the West, meditation was commonly regarded as something mystical and impractical. Today our understanding is completely transformed. The change began when Maharishi introduced a meditation technique that was natural, easy, and something anyone could practice, regardless of their religious or cultural background. He also encouraged scientific research and taught that higher states of consciousness are based on neurophysiological refinement and are innate in each of us.

My first study, using measurements of oxygen consumption, heart rate, skin resistance, blood lactate, and EEG or brain wave activity, verified Maharishi's description of the physiological changes that occur during the Transcendental Meditation® program. The results showed that a unique state of restful alertness is produced by TM—different from our usual states of consciousness, waking, dreaming, and sleeping. These findings suggest the existence of a fourth major state of consciousness, which was described thousands of years ago by many ancient traditions, especially the Vedic tradition of India.

End Anxiety! draws on recent studies, and it is written by a humanist rather than a scientist. As you might expect, the book focuses on human beings instead of data. It examines changes in the lives of people who come to TM® centers suffering from anxiety and other personal problems.

The narrative does not resort to rhetoric or imaginings but uses the language of our time, the language of science. Among other things, it deals with EEG research which indicates that not all meditation techniques are the same. For example, what are the differences in the

EEG and brain imaging findings between Mindfulness and the TM®
technique?

End Anxiety! is an engaging read that highlights decades of practical scientific research on the TM® program, presenting it in a simple,
interesting, and mercifully short volume. I hope that it will help you to
empower and improve your life. Enjoy.

DR. ROBERT KEITH WALLACE
Trustee and Founding President of Maharishi International University,
Chair of Department of Physiology and Health

Preface

Anxiety. Things are going bad, you worry. Things are going okay, you worry. Things are going great, you worry. Worry, fear, depression, angst—they're pretty much the human condition. Sure, there are periods of respite, but not most of the time, not for most of the people. How do you fix it? Success? Family? Sedatives? Therapy? Cognitive behavioral psychology? Religion? What is it with anxiety? What *is* it? It's relentless. Seemingly incurable.

Once upon a time, long ago in the mid-1970s, Maharishi Mahesh Yogi told me something as he was ushering me toward activity away from him and among the rest of humankind. He said: "It will be inspiring to be in the field teaching Transcendental Meditation® [instead of at international headquarters]." For decades, before becoming a full-time teacher, I wondered at that prescription. Perhaps it would be inspiring to my writing, which surely it was. In 2005, when I began point-of-contact teaching with the general public, I learned over and over what in fact he meant. It is inspiring to see from the results of the Transcendental Meditation® program how quickly and completely people recover from even the most crippling stress and anxiety.

Sometimes it seems as if nobody knows how powerful the TM® technique really is. You can't grasp it intellectually, and none of us can fully express it, because the power of the Transcendental Meditation® technique comes "from where speech returns" as Maharishi Mahesh Yogi, the TM® program founder, has put it. The ground state. The infinite. The source.

People who do not actually practice the Transcendental Meditation® technique these days can be especially at a severe disadvantage because of all the talk of many kinds of meditation. The airways are clogged with "meditation" and "yoga" and "being present" until you don't know where to turn for good advice and may just want to shut down the pursuit of this life enhancement altogether. When I was younger and knew little about these practices, I was at a disadvantage, too, before I learned this practice of meditation. Of course I was. Never, until we have tasted it, could we have the slightest idea of the power of the Transcendental Meditation® technique. Once having experienced it, the wonder doesn't cease; at the least, we find possibilities open before us more and more each day.

Doing the Impossible. Instantly.

I wrote this book to toss in my two cents about that power, the unimaginable power, the mind-boggling, totally unexpected and transforming, genuine, train-wreck-correcting power of the Transcendental Meditation® program. I started out wanting to write about anxiety—and this book did become a book about anxiety—the bane of mankind's existence from the lowliest among us to the most exalted in the halls of power. But I found as the pages accumulated that what I wrote was above all a display of the power of the TM® program, which simply could not be confined to the task of dealing with anxiety alone. (Nevertheless, the recovery from fear and loathing and stress and worry that defines anxiety is a dramatic turnaround, a true display of power.)

What is the nature of this power that I want people to know about? It's the power to fix them: I mean to genuinely make them whole in a way they've never imagined, something they've never found in all of the methods that were claimed to make them well. Then, when they are fixed, like a repaired car leaving the shop, they are ready for the true journey that the TM® program provides. We give a vision of the journey, too, the possibilities that come to us as we emerge from the fog of apathy, doubt, and fear.

Helping Train Wrecks

Modern humans can be, without necessarily admitting it, gravely discouraged. Clueless. Hung out to dry, in spite of our best efforts. The beginning of our approach here is to lay down a groundwork based on real people, genuine hat-in-hand visitors to the center for the TM® program, to give a picture of their needs. This is the "before" in the "before and after." We are bound to give a picture of these seekers—so often disillusioned, angry, frustrated, and tired. They are completely fed up with their lives and the attempt to have more joy and satisfaction. These are people, too, who tend not to believe a word of what anyone promises them. "I'm skeptical," they'll say, as if we as teachers would be hearing it for the first time. But the people are real, and their genuineness is engaging. When I tell their stories here, I have of course changed their names. People don't want to remember their pain or be recognized for it.

Also, we look to show the path to recovery, often an instantaneous turnaround but a long-sought journey nonetheless. People come to us covered with the dust of their travels—trips through books of advice or other means of shedding their fear and doubt. They may visit skilled therapists who definitely help them and often send them to learn the TM® technique or perhaps prescribe sedatives. They go wherever their desperation and need to escape may lead them, possibly to drugs and alcohol and unprescribed Adderall, too. You can follow their travels in these pages.

The TM® program is so much more than a stress buster. So much more. Infinitely more. But it's the stress-busting that people want, and this is the book that goes straight to the nub of the matter—their anxiety—and then continues on to the shimmering possibilities that lie ahead for the meditator using the TM® technique.

There is only one better way to experience the transforming effect of the TM® program than to hear the stories of seemingly impossible results of what happened to real people. What is that one way? To experience the TM® technique yourself. In this book we want you to glimpse the potential of a unique procedure for accessing the power of the universe and bringing it into your daily activity. Having glimpsed it, we hope you'll consider engaging in it.

About Science

We tell stories here—success stories. People love these stories but don't always believe them. They view them as fantastical fictions, thinking the writer must have told them selectively, or the featured people must have changed their minds by now, or the writer embellished key points to exaggerate how quickly people transformed. They don't believe the stories, and for that matter, they don't believe much in scientific explanations, either. But science is the best proof we have.

So we talk about data, but in just an easy way. Maharishi Mahesh Yogi, the founder of the TM® program, recognized that we live in an age of science. Science is the one language we can believe and not exactly trust but grudgingly accept when we can't find any deep-seated flaw in it. So, not in isolation and not in a mind-numbing reiterative style, we share with you scientific research supporting the stories of remarkable turnarounds. We've got to. I'm sorry. We try to make it painless, like dentists who try not to hurt us. The experience is not too bad, and it's much needed.

We do the same with documentation, the sometimes mind-stultifying reference material that must accompany the scientific studies so that we know the data is real and not made up. We place brief captions and sources under each chart. But when this doesn't seem enough oomph to satisfy the most demanding readers (since credibility is at stake), proud scholarly readers can turn to additional details about some of the studies in the reference section in the back matter and dive in to their heart's content. But don't feel pressured to go there. It's half intended to be overlooked. For most, it's probably enough that it's written there.

Start Anywhere, But at the Beginning Is Good

So how do you read this book? Dabble around in it. Check out a chapter or two that seem to be in your wheelhouse, namely something that is an issue of your own or a pet peeve or just an area of curiosity. I'd like to suggest that you start with the first chapter where people moan about their aches and pains. You can get a sense of the problem we're looking to address. If you get drawn in, read a little more. The hope, of course, is that you get swept in altogether and slide through page after page, enthralled with the notion that perhaps there truly is a way out of human misery after all.

Eventually, you might come into a center for the TM® program and learn the technique. Once you've done that, you're at the goal, and then you can just enjoy the book and read it to reinforce what you are doing with the meditation. Or, just grumble about something. That's cool, too. We live in a stressed world. We grumble a lot. But thumb around in these pages a little. Why not? You're here, after all. And I have good stories to tell.

Introduction

It was a Sunday in mid-December in the late afternoon at the Hotel Crillon in Paris in 1967. Maharishi had just performed a ceremony in Sanskrit he called The Holy Tradition and taught us to do TM. The purpose of this ceremony (or puja) is to raise the consciousness of the teacher, and from that heightened state a word or sound called a mantra is given to the initiate. The fact that Maharishi himself gave us our mantras was a blessing. I count it as the most special Christmas present I could ever have gotten.

The feeling was one of the deepest relaxation I'd ever experienced, all from a simple, natural, mental technique that was so simple, yet so profound. No wonder research has shown that the metabolism can go down to a level of rest deeper than deep sleep. The effect of this on mind and body is profound.

Life has never-ending challenges, ups and downs, individually and globally. TM is the best way I know of to help you not only to survive but thrive and meet life's challenges with increased intelligence and creativity while benefiting your health and well-being.

Maharishi, in fact, has provided a formula for world peace which can be possible if enough individuals were to practice TM. The group practice of the TM Sidhi program creates enough positivity in the atmosphere to create world peace.

Love, Mike Love
Incline Village, Nevada
May 2022

PART I
Believing Anxiety Is Unfixable

CHAPTER 1

"Helllp!!" Real People, Real Anxiety

"This is what I'm seeing all the time. Anxiety. Panic attacks. Particularly with the autism kids, because they don't have the filters to deal with the stresses. Anxiety is just all over out there. It's a big, BIG problem."

GARY McCARTY, School Psychologist, Los Angeles Unified School District

I am a teacher of the TM® technique. One evening I'm in a roomful of people who have come to our center to hear an introductory talk about the Transcendental Meditation® program—there are about a dozen of them. They express interest through our website, www.tm.org, and we invite them to come in for an introductory session. Nowadays, thanks to Covid-19, we do introductory talks on Zoom, too. "What brings you here?" I ask. We've passed out a list of possible reasons, or they can make their own choices. You know, "better brain functioning," "more self-fulfillment, "greater creativity"—things like that.

"I'm depressed," announces a nicely dressed woman sitting in the front who would make a perfectly good candidate for "nice, regular person of the month." You'd be happy to sit next to her on the bus. You'd happily strike up a conversation and expect to be uplifted. But she's miserable underneath that carefully maintained exterior. Her troubles are anything but ordinary. She has left her job. Her children, though politely supportive, have distanced themselves from her. She's in a complete funk and can barely drag herself through the day or, in this case, to this talk.

Unbearable Grief and Sorrow

"Who's going to top that?" I ask, quite confident that this room of polite, efficiently dressed grown-ups will not be surpassing her reasons for her low spirits. But I am wrong. "The depth of my grief," says the woman next to her. "My son was killed in the crash of a commercial airliner."

In a single day her life went from pride and steadiness with the usual jolts and headaches to post-traumatic stress, sadness, and irreparable regret. I knew people with that kind of loss suffer a gnawing inner wrenching that just never lets up. Many others in a state of grief have shown up for one of our introductory talks—teenagers who have lost a dad, a devoted wife who lost a husband and was depressed for months before she came to one of our introductory meetings on the TM® technique. Among the grief-stricken have been those who lost a cherished dog or cat. They reach a point of feeling that nothing can help them.

"Who would like to speak next?" I ask. A wealthy accountant in his fifties claimed he had no internal sense of who he was. He said he spent his life handling the wealth of others, being their pillar of strength, while having really no idea what his life was about or where it was going. He told us that in spite of appearances to the contrary, he sometimes felt he was a cipher. A fraud. A rich guy living a good life, putting on a front of bring reasonable while wondering how his life had slipped away and what to do to become something more than the nicely-decked-out empty shell he felt he was.

And who was sitting next to him? A medical doctor. But he wasn't currently working as a doctor because he had left the profession to find himself and get himself in order—a burned-out doctor. I contemplated about why we have so many of them. Doctors are the royalty of the modern world, with everyone unquestioningly attributing to them all the knowledge and skills and abilities they often think they don't truly have. But, gosh, this perception of them is so great. I couldn't help thinking that all they have to do is accept the adulation and paychecks and move confidently through the world. Instead, the doctor was clearly miserable and had an enormous gap in his life without the least idea of how to fill it. His therapist wasn't helping him—or not enough.

And so it goes in the life of the instructor of the TM® technique with nearly impossible problems laid at our feet to be repaired more or less instantly. Who are we, you must wonder. What training could we have that would qualify us for that? Perhaps you are thinking,

"Shouldn't psychiatrists be helping these people? Or social workers with lots of experience? Or medical doctors—psychiatrists especially?" Those professionals do help, of course. But still people come to our center to find out about the TM® technique. They are looking for something more.

Phobias, too. Yikes. Can I really help them?

My list of needy folks goes on, not necessarily the people I met at that meeting, but those who attended other meetings. I remember the mindfulness instructor in his seventies who was completely unaccustomed to sitting in the audience instead of teaching everyone else what to do. He was a master of being "present." And besides, he had been "meditating" for thirty years. He was there only because his wife dragged him, and she (also a mindfulness instructor) was there because, in spite of having all the trappings, she wasn't happy. She was anxious, and if you asked her about it, she said her husband was, too.

Occasionally there have been therapists in the audience. One, a paragon of knowingness, felt inside a certain non-knowingness. "If I hear one more person say he wants to be 'present,' I think I'll"—she said, catching herself before finishing the sentence. Or the successful grip (a mechanic who works in the movies) might be there because she knew so many people she admired who did the TM® technique. She would sign up and reserve a spot, only eventually to disappear without starting the program. She made good money, was reasonably comfortable, and wasn't particularly stressed. She wasn't convinced she needed the TM® technique, and she wasn't convinced she didn't, either. She just wasn't as anxious as most of the others.

"I haven't slept for nine years," interjected a participant during a recent meeting. How many things had he tried in that time? How skewed does your physiology become if you don't sleep for so long? Was he exaggerating? He was a successful film producer. A little bit famous. Living the dream.

One wealthy business owner came in, prevailed upon by his wife to attend. Not in his first meeting, but after a few times of being with his teacher of the TM® technique, he stated his main problem. "I can't stand to sit in the window seat on a plane," he said. It made him feel trapped. It brought on a panic attack. He had long since resolved that he simply, under no circumstance, would sit in that place on an airplane. And of course as a CEO he had to travel a lot.

One 22-year-old came in marshalled by his dad. He was a freelance illustrator who was educated and personable and working at home. He wouldn't drive because his anxiety was just too much for him. Hence the presence of his dad, who did the driving.

"My husband is in hospice at home," another confessed. Her shining star, her long-term partner, had been struck with a cruel form of dementia. Have you been close to spouses of people dying from dementia or Parkinson's or late-stage cancer or whatever else might be afflicting their partner? I find that the dying person has often come to terms with this and is relatively at peace. But the supportive partner is exhausted and in torment. The man's wife was there to be helped by me, the teacher of the TM® technique with five months of training. By the way, this is a good time to note it's the technique, not the teacher, that is the main instrument of the change that people come in to find.

But I want to continue with my list of people who attend these meetings. It includes rich realtors. Beautiful people. TV stars. Movie stars. Wait, let's go on. Car salesmen. Car lot owners. We're talking luxury cars, Mercedes and Lexus and BMW. Some teenagers have come to these talks. A polite transsexual came in whose pronoun was "they" and whose mom was very solicitous and understood her child and wanted to ease "their" path in life. Both had some anxiety, but that was understandable given the societal challenges they faced. Builders come to the meetings. Set finders. Set builders. Haberdashers. Used clothing haberdashers. IT specialists. Overwhelmingly rich people. Overwhelmingly broke people. The occasional homeless person. Anybody can suffer from anxiety.

Desperate and Sleepless

Here they were, all on this earth, and aside from the occasional exception of a person who probably wouldn't decide to learn the TM® technique anyway, they were desperate to find a solution. They were pleading, "Someone please help me," hoping against hope that maybe this thing called the TM® technique would bring them some relief. Or, check that. They did not truly think it would help but had enough gas left in the tank to keep trying things, howsoever half-heartedly. Their collective misery was barely concealed, and they had (even the ones who were sometimes happy and well-adjusted) this one thing in common.

And usually they had side effects that went with their stress and anxiety. Insomnia was rife. Occasionally a person arrived who slept well, but this was rare and usually half-hearted; that is, someone might sleep fitfully and not deep enough to have a restful sleep. At other times they slept too deeply, using sleep as an escape from depression. Meanwhile other things in their life lacked attention as they slid further and further into a sinkhole of despair.

Physical challenges were commonplace. Some people were just simply in pain and had sometimes been like this for years. Perhaps from an aching back. Or from headaches. Digestive problems. Lupus. Early onset signs of dementia. Oh, and cardiovascular problems. And cancer, often as a one- or two-time "survivor."

And the many addictive habits of the American middle class were on display. Alcohol was the most common addiction but far from the only one. For some it was marijuana. Cocaine had a few adherents. Most didn't want to own up to it publicly, but a sex addict would show up now and then. Workaholics and tireless overworked people going nowhere in particular were there. An entertainment lawyer, successful (as in having many clients and a good income) was trembling and distracted and seemed to be searching everywhere for a way out. He didn't start the program, so I couldn't help him. He was completely overburdened and miserable in what you would think is a dream job for an attorney (and I did think that because I have a son who's an attorney).

No wonder people complain about the traffic on the freeways in LA. It's not the congestion. It's not the glut of cars that turn the road into a parking lot where people inch along. It's the barely contained fear and outrage and despair of the drivers. On the freeway there it is, all that stress compressed into a paved area 100 feet wide and stretching interminably into the future. Sometimes it seems that the congested traffic itself could just erupt, inexplicably erupt.

In the time we live in, there are many reliable sources to confirm what we all know anyway: that stress is bustin' out all over, and for most people shows no signs of letting up. Facts and statistics in the chart below show that anxiety is rampant in our country.

As a teacher of the TM® technique, I often hear troubled people describe their suffering. The plea for help is laid at my feet, but to look to me as a source of healing seemed absurd in the sense of the extremity of the demand and the hopelessness of a cure coming from anyone with just five months of training as a teacher of the Transcendental Meditation® program. How was I to help these people? And, if I could help one of the admittedly depressed men, could I then turn around

Anxiety
The Scope of the Problem

- Anxiety disorders are the most common mental health problem in the United States.
- Anxiety afflicts 40 million U.S. adults—about 18% of the population.
- Anxiety disorders develop from a complex set of risk factors, including genetics, brain chemistry, personality, and life events.
- Anxiety costs the U.S. more than $42 billion a year, almost one-third of the country's $148 billion total mental health bill.
- Anxiety increases the risk of chronic diseases, such as coronary heart disease.
- Anxiety motivates people to smoke and drink, which further impairs health.

Reference: Anxiety and Depression Association of America. Facts and Statistics, 2015; Available from: http://www.adaa.org/about-adaa/press-room/facts-statistics.

and help the woman who was grieving for the loss of her partner or the one in the full throes of an identity crisis? I knew perfectly well it was not "I" (not me at all, really) but this TM® technique that would help them, even transform them. But seeing the complexity of their problems and their history of failed attempts to solve them, I thought it seemed downright grandiose to think (as I did and as every teacher of the TM® technique does) that I could be of real help.

Anxiety. Oh, my God. It's everywhere. People have tried everything, and the only reason they try the next thing and the next is that in spite of everything life tends to have a slight upward trajectory even if it often carries us, relentlessly, to more and more disappointments, fear, pain, and anxiety. Do we just put on a face, live the lie, and ride things out for the day?

What would happen to these people when they learned the TM® technique? I'll tell you in a bit, but seeing them when they come in, a little reluctant, almost sheepish, you have to wonder what anyone can do. Does anyone completely escape from this condition? Is there any way out? Or did Kafka have it right? We're cockroaches, hiding in the dark, living in fear, holding out against that inevitable moment when a foot appears out of nowhere and squashes us. I mean, let me tell you about Samuel Johnson. Oprah. Abe Lincoln. People report seeing Lincoln's ghost around the White House. That's how bad things must have gotten for him, if ghosts are perhaps earthbound spirits consumed with stress. And he's probably the greatest historical figure in the history of the nation. Even the great can't seem to sidestep anxiety.

CHAPTER 2

No One Escapes Anxiety

"Abraham Lincoln fought clinical depression all his life, and if he were alive today, his condition would be treated as a 'character issue'—that is, as a political liability."

JOSHUA WOLF SHENK, "Lincoln's Great Depression,"
The Atlantic, October 2005

One day, when I was being a good PhD in English and simply wanted to round out my education and continue it, for that matter, I thought I would read on my Kindle (for free, as it turned out) some works of the Dean of English Letters, the honorable seventeenth century icon, Samuel Johnson, and in the process read the greatest single biography ever written—Boswell's *Life of Johnson*. Now Johnson, you have to understand, is an ultimate figure. A God. You don't just read him as a student, you pore over him, memorize him, assimilate him as entirely as you can into your own life, knowing you can never attain his stratospheric stature. Of course not.

Legendary Anxiety

What tormented this living treasure throughout his life and took away so much of the pleasure of his lofty station in life and in letters? Mr. Boswell called it "hypochondria," but this has a different meaning today; specifically, it's an "illness anxiety disorder" when a person is overly concerned about health and imagines physical ailments that don't exist. Today we refer to the mental condition that was so familiar to Boswell as a generalized anxiety disorder (GAD), commonly described as "intense anxiety often accompanied by severe depression."

What hope is there when our ultimate role models, our highest achievers, the standard setters and standard bearers, are themselves victims of the relentless, harping demons that we, their students, are trying through them to avoid?

Realistically, we can infer that anxiety has always been there, if we want to think of anxiety as the fear we experience when there is no immediate threat. Nah, let's go all the way. It's the fear we live with intermittently or on a daily basis depending on our circumstance.

How did cave men keep from living in constant fear when there could have been a hungry saber-toothed tiger in the neighborhood and diseases like cholera and pneumonia and smallpox could strike unannounced and wreak havoc? In any case, they knew they weren't going to live very long, and everyone is likely to be a bit anxious as they live out their final days on Earth. How about Greek and Roman periods? There is speculation that Julius Caesar, Emperor of Rome in the first century before Christ, may have had epilepsy and certainly had plenty to worry about in a life that ended with his dear and trusted Brutus, of "et tu, Brute?" fame, orchestrating his stabbing.

What about the lives of ordinary people living at that time? There was the threat of invasion by the Romans, generally carried out before too long, and the fear of a life as a slave to the Romans. How about the conquering soldiers themselves? They lived a rather dangerous life, had to be away from their families for long periods, and worked under imperious and demanding leaders. Surely anxiety came into their lives, followed after a battle with growing post-traumatic stress.

What was the life of a serf in the Middle Ages? Barely enough to eat. High rates of infant mortality. Thoughtless and cruel managers. Dysentery, malaria, diphtheria, flu, typhoid, smallpox, and leprosy striking out of the blue with no effective treatments. Many on the planet were threatened with invasion and a life of slavery. If they weren't fearful, they should have been. It wasn't called "The Dark Ages" for nothing.

How were things for those romantic pirates on the high seas? Danger lurked from every mast coming up over the horizon and every bit of land they might sight, not to mention the risk of peril from their comrades and leaders and from the formal military of those countries like England that they preyed on. Ah, the life of a pirate was no field day.

In Shakespeare's time, Bedlam was the name of the London lunatic asylum, and it certainly did not lack for occupants. "As flies to wanton boys are, we to the Gods," laments King Lear in the play of his name, and he surely suffered from depression no matter how much circumstance may have made his reactions quite appropriate. I mean, you take care of your daughters, and they take you for granted and leave you to rot? He should have expected it, and his anxiety was hardly baseless, but it was dramatic and real. Hamlet? Lady Macbeth? Othello? Pain and misery. Cruel fate.

Later scholars and researchers look at our greatest geniuses and see clouds of trouble. Take Van Gogh, of course. Every schoolchild learns that he cut off his own ear, and he ended his life at age 37. Both Beethoven and Mozart had difficulties; Mozart possibly suffered from Tourette syndrome. In his *Leviathan* in the 17th century, Thomas Hobbes describes human life as solitary, nasty, brutish, and (the greatest hurt of all) short. The specter of death hangs over us the entire time.

Even Lincoln?

Abraham Lincoln, possibly the most idolized of all American presidents, reportedly suffered long bouts of depression even before the trauma of the Civil War. And what about ordinary people alive at the time of Lincoln? They faced conscription into a bloody war against people who looked and thought much like them at a time when a large population of Americans was living as slaves. Stephen Crane's *The Red Badge of Courage* memorializes the plight of the Civil War soldier caught in brutal, meaningless conflict. Mortality struck on the battlefield, and it struck in childbirth. Families had to endure not only the loss of infants; their children often died.

Charles Dickens (say it isn't so) reportedly suffered depression, even severe depression and perhaps bipolar disorder. While he was enthralling the world with *David Copperfield* and *A Tale of Two Cities* and the transformative story of Ebenezer Scrooge, he apparently was not living without disturbances in his own mind that interfered with enjoying the pleasure of his fame and fortune.

Jump to modern times. It is not wholly surprising, I suppose, that clinicians would conclude that the hero to so many alternative thinkers, author Jack Kerouac, had mental disorders. Perhaps the mental conditions prompted him to go "on the road" himself and later create the classic with that name. Please, not Jack Kerouac as an example for anxiety disorder. But alas, probably he, too, was afflicted.

And the one other most beloved book of the time, *The Catcher in the Rye*, came from the author J.D. Salinger, who certainly did not come out to participate in a public life to enjoy the adulation so many had for him. J.D., the great, who broke down centuries of pretension with remarks like Holden Caulfield's observation that "He started handling my exam paper like it was a turd or something." If Mr. Salinger was comfortable within himself, then where was he? Of course, no one maintains that he was comfortable. He was a veritable misanthrope.

Ernest Hemingway, whose old man at sea sees his great capture devoured before his eyes before he reaches shore, put himself out of his misery with suicide. Later on, so did the admired writer Hunter Thompson, a journalist and bestselling author who loved drugs and rode with the Hells Angels but whose suicide told his fans that perhaps he didn't have the answer, either, and must have been miserable.

And what about anxiety for the ordinary person of the 1950s when conformity was the norm, a nine-to-five job was sheer necessity, and staying in a marriage you disliked and a job you hated was what people would describe as "just how it is done"? *Peyton Place* pictured the best you could do to escape that captivity of everyday life in conformity. *Lady Chatterley's Lover* did the same. Good luck. Out of the frying pan and into the fire. You might escape all the rest of it, but you couldn't hide from your own tormenting brain. Well, books like Dale Carnegie's *How to Stop Worrying and Start Living* were bestsellers for a reason.

And what dominated the academic and philosophical thinking of the time? Existentialism. Camus treated audiences to the vision of a world where the plague had struck and pain and misery were the rule of the time. Camus's hero in *L'Étranger* refused to go to his mother's funeral. Sad. Extreme. The son probably brought her a lot of angst. But she probably expected it. Sartre underlined his countrymen's thinking and assured all that there was just "No Exit." Meanwhile, off stage, the Beatniks were howling, pretty much in despair, the only break being the sardonic witticisms of a cynical Lenny Bruce. It doesn't seem right to mention him without quoting him. I found this joke on funnycomediansquotes.com:

> "I won't say ours was a tough school, but we had our own coroner. We used to write essays like: What I'm going to be if I grow up."

Oprah, the Rock

Now, a more contemporary list on the website WebMD highlights its collection of anxious famous folks with none other than the rock for the rest of us, the counselor Oprah Winfrey. Who else does it offer up to disillusion and disturb us? Stephen Colbert, a great source of escape through laughter, knows something firsthand about panic attacks. Howie Mandel, who judges others in *America's Got Talent*, apparently is more than familiar with the agony the show's candidates are going through. Whoopi Goldberg, whose fame and acting career I once read came with little effort, nevertheless suffers pangs and doubts during her life of great success.

And we think of the brilliant, enigmatic Brian Wilson, the co-founder of The Beach Boys. Maybe life isn't always a beach. Kevin Love, the nephew of Mike Love, another Beach Boy, came out to the National Basketball Association and his fans about his problems with anxiety. I saw it on camera. In the midst of a game this goliath of a man puts his palm on his head and kneels down, overcome by anxiety. The other team can't get him, but his inner demons can bring him down. Wait. This next one can't be right. I'm adding here "Barbara Streisand." She's our comfort. Our assurance. When the going gets tough, we turn to her music to reaffirm that "the way we were" was once idyllic and grand and remind ourselves it could be that way again.

What am I saying here? Am I saying that that a roomful of stressed-out, sometimes desperate and hopeless people who might show up for an introductory lecture on the TM® technique are a microcosm of human life, and not just life as it is today but life a thousand and ten thousand and a hundred thousand years ago? Am I saying basically that if I could fix the broken people who had come to me that night of the lecture I would be righting the human condition, now and for all time?

Yes, in a sense, I would be saying that, except that it wouldn't be *me* doing it. I'd be just the instrument, the middleman, applying an ancient knowledge discovered and rediscovered by fully enlightened sages who from time to time grace the Earth with their presence and save us from the misery we've fallen into.

But, yeah, as the instrument, I would be offering a simple practice that I was saying would fix them by eliminating whatever was wrong. Depressed? Maybe you can turn on the lights inside. Grieving? Maybe you can be happy again someday. Sick? The body heals itself, even when we don't know what's wrong, as in the case of fibromyalgia and the sweepingly named "chronic fatigue syndrome," which often seems to translate as "We don't know what's really wrong, but you're very tired."

And what if this one over here is an addict—to alcohol or drugs or sex or, as some would say, to just about anything and everything. Am I telling them I would fix that, too? (No, not me. Not me. But what I'm saying would work is this ancient, funny-sounding, frequently over-looked method—the Transcendental Meditation® technique.)

In my all-encompassing statement, am I saying that I will teach something that, whatever is wrong, will fix it no matter how extreme the problem is or how long it has been there? Well, let's not go completely overboard. The distressed woman whose her husband was in the late stages of dementia wouldn't allow me to attempt to teach him the TM® program. She was so upset about his decline that she couldn't visualize how this might comfort him. Of course, incurable conditions like extreme dementia, severe lupus or Parkinson's disease, and cancers at late stages are not suddenly going to abate. But the TM® technique, for absolutely any adversity, will make very ill persons feel more upbeat, sleep better, and have more strength to handle their difficulties. And it can also fix a lot of things.

And I am definitely saying that it will help with anxiety. In cases where the worry is completely unfounded, it just may eliminate the severe feelings of stress altogether, removing an ongoing source of torment in the person's life and, as someone said after two months of practicing the TM® technique, "giving them their life back." In instances where there is a long-term source of the anxiety, such as a surgery looming or a diagnosis of an incurable illness, the source of stress is likely to keep renewing the anxiety even as the TM® technique helps it. Fear in this situation is natural and serves a purpose. Sometimes we should be scared. Real danger does lurk out there, but usually not most of the time. And it's been proven that practicing the technique can help to bring calm and even some peace to a person who has been devastated by a terrible experience.

Putting aside the most extreme situations, yeah, that's what I definitely want to say: "You've come to the right place to get help for your anxiety. Schedule a session on Saturday, bring in some flowers and a couple pieces of fruit, and finally you will get relief." The look on their faces tells it all. "And you're going to sell me a bridge, too, right?" Nobody believes it from just hearing about it. Besides, they've been scouring the web and doctor's offices and the bookstores and everything they can bring up on their Kindles. Nothing has worked. It seems *unfixable*.

CHAPTER 3

It's Obviously Unfixable

"He cried in a whisper at some image, at some vision—he cried out
twice, a cry that was no more than a breath—'The horror!'"

(Kurtz's final words in JOSEPH CONRAD'S *Heart of Darkness*,
summing up his view of the nature of life. This was repeated
by MARLON BRANDO in the movie *Apocalypse Now*.)

There are lots of reasons that people would doubt that meditation can
work as an elixir for anxiety, many reasons why people who come for
help would expect they'd end up walking away feeling disappointed.
Consider the magnitude of the challenge. If everybody has anxiety
(okay, almost everybody), and if everybody has always had it, and if
everybody has been trying to fix it every day of their lives, then face
it—it's unfixable.

1. **First of all, it's just the way life is. It's not always great.
   Stuff happens. We're not static.**

Yes, stuff happens. The first time I saw that phrase in its more vulgar
version was on a bumper sticker in Davenport, Iowa. Middle America. Vanilla life. Leave-it-to-Beaver land, where you might think nothing much happens. Maybe you lose your pen. Maybe school closes for
a day because of the snow. Yet there was a haunting certainty about
that phrase on the bumper sticker. In Davenport, or anywhere else, you
don't just get a free pass and go happily on your way.

There's your family. Just when you were going to reach for the last
brownie, someone else is eating it. Your dog dies. Your father dies.
A tree branch falls through the back-porch roof—your roof, not the
neighbor's—*yours*. You don't get promoted and have to struggle along
as an assistant HR Manager in the packaging company instead of the

19

manager. You do get promoted, but packaging hits a serious lull as everyone starts selling their products open to the air; and your assignment is to lay off one third of the staff, most of whom you love dearly and see at the supermarket frequently.

Life is always progressing, which means it is always throwing stuff at us, both good and bad, and it isn't just small bad stuff either but death and firings and disabilities and unwanted pregnancies and tax audits and dented fenders and home break-ins and behind-your-back cavil from the girl you thought was your best friend. Challenges. Failures. Bankruptcies. That's the first reason that worry is unfixable. Stuff happens. Get used to it.

2. Second of all, you can't always put the whole mess on someone else.

Finger pointing can seem a great idea. Just blame somebody else. Government officials love to do that. "I know that the water supply is exhausted, and we have to ration. But it's not my fault. My predecessor did not plan properly." The trouble with finger pointing is that the other person points back. "I have always had a wonderful record of water management, and I cautioned you about electing somebody who didn't." The first finger pointer replies, "Oh, no you didn't." And the mudslinging continues, contaminating everyone and getting nowhere.

It's the old tar baby story. You slap the tar baby to fix the problem. You're stuck with one hand. You strike with the other hand, with your feet, with your head. You are stuck, and the problem is not the least bit ameliorated. It's worse. You had a problem, but still have the problem after you went after it. Even if you sometimes fix a problem, soon it's just back to point one. New stuff happens.

3. Third, you hate the things everybody recommends for fixing it.

They go prancing around offering advice, and then you find out that they don't really follow it themselves. There are names for it. "Mansplaining" is one of them. People pose as experts, but half the time they don't really know anything. The other half of the time they are almost as capable as you are. They just happen to be lucky this time that something happened to you and not to them.

"Oh, you got audited by the IRS. No big deal. That happened to me once. Just hire H&R Block." "I already tried that—" you start to retort, but what's the use? They don't care. They aren't listening. "Not my problem," they're thinking. Advice is cheap and worth what you pay for it. So, we get in the habit of not listening to what might be helpful advice. And the time we did decide to listen, we got in deeper and deeper and at the end found out we have to pay for it one way or another. By now we are inured and just let all the advice bounce off us like little nerf balls.

4. **Fourth, you just don't have time to drop back and try to fix it. You're *in* it.**

You are too busy. You're working. You go to your job and do your assignment (at this time evaluating loan applications and making recommendations). You do this all day and get really tired and feel fed up. At evening time, you need a break. You have a small cocktail, a diluted Manhattan (and this is not at all because you're addicted), and then you want dinner, and then there's an episode of *Real Housewives* you think will give you a little respite before you fall asleep in front of the TV, and soon it's morning and you have to go to your job. Since there's no time to find a solution to the problem that's worrying you, it seems better just to accept that you're going to go on worrying. Even if you did happen to fix the problem, something else will come up. If you weren't so busy, maybe, yes, you could fix it. But you don't have the time, and the more you put it off, the worse it gets and the more it weighs on you.

5. **You don't think the precedents for fixing the problem work for you.**

We almost always feel like the problem is our particular problem and not something where we can study the precedents. But your situation no doubt has earlier occurrences of similar happenings. There is nothing new under the sun. But somehow we tend to feel that our particular instance of a dilemma is ours alone. Maybe it's something simple, like you need $220 for a car payment. What do other people do in this circumstance? Well, they borrow from a friend. Or they borrow on a credit card. Or pick up an odd job that pays that much. Sure, there are precedents, but in the heat of the moment we don't tend to seek them out. You've exhausted financial support from your friends. You dread adding to credit card debt. Whatever good options you may have you are too stressed out to see.

6. Fixing it often backfires. Better to just leave it alone.

People aren't grateful. Suppose your son accidentally broke another 14-year-old's glasses, and the mom of the other child asks you to pay the $160 for the glasses, and you do it. You pay it. Is everything then all better? Not necessarily. First of all, the mom will think that you are a pushover for other demands and may make them. You may very much need the $160 yourself to help pay off the income tax penalty you know you have to pay, and if you don't pay it you face fresh penalties and more worry. In any case, whether or not there are any other repercussions, the person will not be grateful for what you did. You are out the $160, and you have scored no points with anyone else by doing it. The great Dale Carnegie himself, author of *How to Stop Worrying and Start Living*, says it flatly. "Expect ingratitude." Or, to fill out this sixth point even more fully, expect repercussions that may be worse than the problem you were deftly looking to fix in the first place. Just leave it, go to work, come home to dinner, and worry about it all day.

7. Nothing has worked so far.

Because nothing seems to work, the smart thing is just to become cynical and plan for the worst. You keep your dignity, and you are right as far as anyone can tell. Maybe you can get some mileage out of being cynical about the whole thing. A tree fell on your house. There are a lot of comic possibilities in that. "I was planning to take that tree down anyway. Good riddance." "I need the firewood." "I hated the squirrel living in that tree. Serves him right." "The kids wanted a treehouse in it, and I didn't." "I needed a remodel in that part of the house. Now I have no choice but to do it." "This is a great story to tell my sister in

San Francisco. Pass me my phone." Maybe that's it. Smoothly make light of the problem, and just go back to the office and pore over some loan applications all day.

Having problems is a permanent state that's just unfixable, and deep down inside we know that and hence we worry about them. Oh, sure, you think you can solve your problems, and maybe sometimes in some instances you can a little bit, but then there will just be new problems to send you into another round of worry and self-doubt and depression. On their own level, on the surface, problems beget problems beget problems. You're hamstrung, and you know it. Of course they're unsolvable. And if they're not they might as well be, because life is sure to throw another obstacle your way that's even bigger. And probably even more unfixable.

And all those difficulties exacerbate the most unfixable problem of all: the worry itself. Don't even bother to try to make it better. If anyone wants to tell you they have a way to stop the worrying, don't listen. If someone tells you they have the only way to solve worrying, especially don't listen to this. Life has a certain momentum. Inertia really. It holds us back from changing things. We just would rather not go there, thank you.

CHAPTER 4

Don't Wanna Try to Fix It Anyway

"I sat awhile in perfect silence, rallying my stunned faculties. Immediately it occurred to me that my ears had deceived me, or Bartleby had entirely misunderstood my meaning. I repeated my request in the clearest tone I could assume; but in quite as clear a one came the previous reply, 'I would prefer not to.'"

Bartleby the Scrivener by HERMAN MELVILLE

Here we are, then, with that roomful (a world full, really) of people with serious problems like the ones I introduced to you, and almost all of their troubles result in one thing—anxiety. Fixing those anguishing situations is highly unlikely, and, anyway, when you fix one, others come along. Fixing the overriding problem of anxiety is particularly unlikely, and everyone in the room is well aware of that. Everybody has the dilemma of worry. Most people have always had that problem. Anxiety persists, in part because of a history of failure in fixing problems, in part because a direct analysis shows it to be unfixable, and lastly because those seeking relief have found anxiety in their own experience to be the last survivor.

If you stand before a group invited to learn about TM to offer what you claim to be a solution, you're in trouble before you even open your mouth. If there is a solution to anxiety, where has it been all their lives? You look out at a room full of implacable faces. All seem noncommittal. Some appear doubtful, and here and there is some barely restrained hostility. They have come, so there is a sliver of an opening to reach them, but it is only a sliver.

Never Say Something is "the Only" Solution

Still, as a teacher of TM, you can offer a solution, and why not? Everybody always wants to help, and now you are another such person. Here is where everything escalates. You are not just offering *a* solution. You have the outright daring—chutzpah really—to be offering the *only* solution. You may not even say that, though I often do say that, but you are out at sea without a life raft when offering the *only* solution to an unfixable problem.

1. First of all, many people think you are probably delusional to take such a stance. The likeable thing to do is to gently offer "*a*" solution, one of many possibilities. People can tolerate that. But people don't like something being the *only* thing that will work—or someone being the *only* one who is able to do something, such as "He's the only one who can climb that wall." "The only one who can walk and skate-board at the same time." "The only one who can solve this equation." Whatever "only one" you might be offering, they are right there with the retort: "No, he isn't.

2. If they do something already, even if it's not working, they aren't about to do what you are offering. ("Our plates are full, man. Don't ask us to do one more thing.") You're up against it, then. You can just try to turn to logic to justify yourself.

3. If you present the argument that if nothing has worked so far, and if they have seen so many possible fixes that have failed, there can't be that many left. If anything works, it is probably the only thing that works. But such reasoning bites its own tail and is hard to sort out.

4. You need a new seed to yield a new crop. What is needed, you suggest, is the principle of the second element: bringing light to move the darkness instead of attempting to fight the darkness on its level. All the obstacles that hold people back from solving their worry (all the issues from depression to lack of a sense of self) come from addressing the problem on its own level. We don't solve worry by solving the problem we are anxious about, you suggest. We need to

solve the problem of worry itself, not the broken faucet or the late train or the unruly child or whatever difficulty they are worrying about. You ask them, "Do you keep bumping into things in the dark?" Don't move things around to clear a path. Don't avoid the room. Don't stack things up. *Turn on the lights.*

Maybe the suggestion of bringing in a second element gets a slight inner nod of acceptance from some of the audience. But you are dealing here with a problem they are wildly motivated to solve and have never solved so far, like twisting and twisting a Rubik's Cube that defiantly and with a bit of a sneer never comes out right. You are basically suggesting, "Throw it out and get a new Rubik's Cube. Never touch it again."

Wouldn't it be great, you say, if you could solve your worry that way? Just throw it out? Do a meditation that doesn't wrestle with it but just ignores it? You can go further with good evidence and offer encouraging stories. "I taught someone who was so stressed out he had to . . ." And then tell them how happy she became after learning the technique. You can register a few stories that people relate to. But they privately think the solution is impossible.

Yawn . . . Science? No Thanks.

Now it's time to offer up the methodology of good science. Scientists have measured the levels of anxiety in people before and after they meditate. They look at something like the stress hormone or blood pressure or heart rate or breathing rate or brain waves or all of the physical indicators of stress. They measure them, reliably, before meditation, and they measure them after meditation. They do hard science, not just passing out forms to people who insist, "Oh, yes, it is good for me." They submit the results for review by the highest caliber of scientists in the same field as the experiment. And they publish them.

Scientific research can inspire some confidence, but you know it's not going to win the day. Not really. If it did, the whole world would be practicing this easy solution to stress and strain. Nothing really works for sure. What may open the door to some receptivity is the presence of the speaker, a calm presence of someone who speaks with ease. A worried presenter has a hard time convincing people that the technique he teaches actually eliminates worry.

A person's own easy presence is the *sine qua non* for a speaker giving his or her case against worry. They appear to have something. They themselves do not seem to be faking their calm. When Maharishi gave his first presentations to audiences in India in 1957, one man said to him, "I have no idea what you said. But whatever you are offering, I want it." And one other thing, the most telling of all, is the outright desperation of many in the audience. "I don't believe you, but I'll try anything once."

On that flimsy basis alone, on the basis of the worried visitor's unreliable perception that the speaker appears to be calm, comes the willingness to go on a tiny bit further against the overwhelming possibility that this, like all other solutions for worrying, is a load of hooey. For such an implacable problem with a long history of tormenting people, optimistic would-be fixers have tried many, many, things—and almost all of them sounded like they could end anxiety. Their bookshelves bend under the weight of all the self-help books.

PART II

Touting Everyday Solutions for Everyday Anxiety

CHAPTER 5

Books: Rewire Your Brain, Et Al.

"This above all—to thine own self be true,
And it must follow, as the night the day,
Thou canst not then be false to any man.
Farewell. My blessing season this in thee!"

> In SHAKESPEARE's *Hamlet*, Polonius speaking to
> his son Laertes, who dies in the end

Ya gotta love those peppy self-help speeches like the one from Polonius. But, as Shakespeare rather cynically suggests, the words don't really help the listener. He puts the words in the mouth of a known fop and the recipient of the advice does not fare well. Lots of us go through a phase of reading self-help books, often in high school or earlier. When the going gets tough, we may turn to them. Okay, fine. Get some professional help. That is, order a book on your Kindle or just read things on the web about getting over worry. The help is there. The Positivity Blog is right there ready to help you:

"Worry never robs tomorrow of its sorrow, it only saps today of its joy."
—LEO F. BUSCAGLIA

"Worry often gives a small thing a big shadow."
—Swedish Proverb

Just Set Up a Worry Period

There's some advice, really great advice, from the website HealthGuide on how to handle your worry:

"Rather than trying to stop or get rid of an anxious thought, give yourself permission to have it, but put off dwelling on it until later."

Their first three tips begin this way:

1. "Create a 'worry period.'" Choose a set time and place for worrying.

2. "Write down your worries."

3. "Go over your 'worry list' during the worry period."

Suppose you've been sentenced to jail, but you do not have to report for a week. So instead of thinking, "Oh, God, I'm so claustrophobic." "My reputation is shot. Good luck having a career in business as an ex-con." "What about my pills? I need to take seven a day. Will they be good about my pills?" "I hate to bring up sex, but I really hope jail isn't like what I've seen in the movies." Instead of thinking things like this, put off thinking about it until, oh, five o'clock. (It's only 6 a.m.) Just write them down in a list:

1. "Oh, God, I'm claustrophobic."

2. "My reputation is shot. Good luck having a career in business as an ex-con."

3. "What about my pills? I take seven a day. Will they be good about my pills?"

4. "I hate to bring up sex, but I really hope jail isn't like what I've seen in the movies."

Then, not having worried all day, go over your list at 5 o'clock and you'll probably find out the following:

1. "You're not that claustrophobic."

2. "You're so charming. You'll turn your ex-con status to advantage."

3. "They lock up pills and give them to you on schedule. You'll be better off."

4. "The movies always exaggerate things for effect."

There you go. You're off to the races. Take that wisdom to heart. Write down your worries. Meet with yourself about them at a fixed time. Great plan.

Everybody loves motivational books. At least a little bit. They're fun. They're peppy. They just sound so true. Usually, truth be told, we love them for somebody else to read. But those upbeat, happy advice-givers have thrived for years. Gosh, the first motivational book is probably the Bible itself. A quick search indicates that *As a Man Thinketh* by James Allen, published in 1903, is an early motivational book. There sure is some great motivation from Shakespeare—"To thine own self be true." The irony is almost cruel as he gives the words from the foolish Polonius, but there the words stand, nevertheless.

You take advice from books and try to tell yourself that none of those negative things you're thinking are going to happen. That's step one in battling anxiety. "That toast was multigrain. It won't make me fat. It's good for me." "Johnny is not going to get kicked out of school. He's good citizen of the week." "I have no reason to suspect my husband of having an affair. When would he be doing it? I'm always with him." "I've got at least five layers of protection between me and being on the street with a shopping cart. Maybe six. Sure, it happens, but it's an extremely low probability for me."

You read, take advice, and apply it to yourself. You reassure yourself. Maybe, extending the pattern a little, you talk to a friend or your spouse, who maybe gets an indulgent look and even tells you, "You worry about nothing that's real." Know what? You can't say why it doesn't work, but talking yourself out of your fretting and misery just doesn't work. Your brain prattles on, tormenting you like a bunch of furies. You know that it will keep doing that even when you try to sleep at night, and then you worry, "Oh, no, I won't be able to sleep tonight, and then I'll be grouchy tomorrow," and before long your mind has you right back there sleeping in the abandoned grocery cart under a bridge.

Go to the Dean of the anti-worry heroes, Dale Carnegie. He's there for you. In *How to Stop Worrying and Start Living* he says, "The best possible way to prepare for tomorrow is to concentrate with all your intelligence, all your enthusiasm, on doing today's work superbly today." "Yes," you tell yourself. "Of course. I get it. Focus on today. I'm off to my desk and taking in a few fresh orders. Sure, that's it. I'm on it. But what if there are no orders there? What if they order something we don't have? What if there are complaints in there? This will cause bills. Yes, there will be bills."

Just Rewire Your Brain

Hordes of books clamber to rescue us from our misery, with their sheer number being testament to how persistent and persnickety worry truly is. Here are a few titles you'd likely find helpful:

- *The Anxiety & Worry Workbook* by two experts in cognitive behavior therapy—and with worksheets, no less. Activities and exercises. Something to get your mind engaged in something other than worry.

- *Overcoming Worry & Generalised Anxiety Disorder, 2nd Edition*—recently published, fancy, and with British spelling. Long and technical. But it brings hope.

- *When Panic Attacks* by David D. Burns, MD—Clever and catchy. Worth a read, for sure.

- *Overcoming Anxiety: A Self-Help Guide Using Cognitive Behavioral Techniques*—I bet it works for some people. Give it a shot. The Cognitive Behavioral Techniques are probably mindfulness, which we have a bit to say about later.

- *The Worry Cure: Seven Steps to Stop Worry from Stopping You*—Bold. And clever with that play on the word "stop." Maybe this one will help.

- *Rewire Your Anxious Brain: How to Use the Neuroscience of Fear to End Anxiety, Panic, and Worry*—Wow. Neuroscience. Mankind is nothing if not persistent. But it's easy to read and clearly explains the neurobiology of troubling psychological conditions.

You'd think the whole search for relief would end right there with reading self-help books. Much of their advice is so solid. It's systematic with techniques you can apply every day, every hour if you want to. Like writing down those worries. Assaulting them with your newfound brain power.

What could be wrong with the self-help books? Well, something must be, given how many people end up still looking for something after reading lots of them. Here's a starter for what might be missing. The advice is intellectual. That is, it's on the level of the thinking. Well, God bless it, but the intellect is pretty much a secondhand tool. It blows this way and that. You have to keep applying its little advice. "Robbing today of its joy." Then five minutes later you apply it again. "Robbing today of its joy." Wait, was it "robbing" or "stealing?" Intellect isn't a powerful enough tool.

I was renting a camper van for a few weeks, and it had some books in it—namely three technical books on fishing and one self-help book with pithy, clever advice on calming down. There it was, the 21st century *How to Stop Worrying and Start Living* in true millennial language. I like it. Here's some of what we find in there, summarized on Amazon's listing for the book:

- "The Four Faces of Freaking Out—and Their Flipsides"

- "How to accept what you can't control"

- "Productive Helpful Effective Worrying (PHEW)"

- "The Three Principles of Dealing With It"

- "And much more!"

The author, Sarah Knight, is a great writer—glib and catchy and funny. And the advice is good, too. It just isn't enough.

So, sure, we do the right thing and find books. And they help. God bless them. But somehow, for those people in the room week after week for an introduction to the Transcendental Meditation® program, they haven't worked enough. To hear their stories of misery, they haven't worked at all. Something about reading in itself is not fundamental enough for the brain. The worry eats away at the edges of everything and soon takes over altogether. Books work a little. You feel a teensy bit better. But they are like trying to kill an elephant with a fly swatter. Maybe if, instead of reading, you get an app on your phone to solve your worry. Apps are the latest thing. It's amazing how much you can compress into one program on your powerful little iPhone or Android phone. Yeah, that must be it. Get an app for worrying.

CHAPTER 6

Apps and More Apps:
Eternal Internet Meditations

"It's the most remarkable thing. I was having anxiety attacks every day, at least five times a week. Since starting the TM® technique [two weeks ago] I've had no attacks at all. It's incredible. It's a subtle change, but it's real.

I've tried other meditations. It wasn't restful. Mindfulness. Even guided meditations. My brain was still going nuts. It didn't feel very different from when I was not meditating. So, I didn't continue with them."

SILENA SMITH-SHAMEY, Los Angeles

What's the miracle device of the 21st century? The phone. No question. And what gives the phone its remarkable power? Not phone calling, certainly. The old monopoly AT&T with its landlines did the calling better. No, what makes phones so smart, of course, is apps. If you want to do something, do it with an app. Once you have the app, it's done. You don't have to actually use the app. It's there. Your conscience is clear. You're up to date.

Take, for example, the wonderfully named "WhatsApp." It's a cool messaging app from Meta. You just put it on your phone. Free long-distance phone calls, with video. What's not to like? If you have friends who use What's App, you use it, too. If you don't have those friends, well, it's nice to have it on your phone. Over 2 billion people in more than 180 counties also use it.

And TikTok, one of the fastest-growing social media apps in the United States, quickly out of the gate surged past its first billion users. Instagram. Zoom. The mighty Facebook itself whose company is, of course, Meta. There is a deluge of apps. You're really not in our century if you don't have a load of apps. Uber, for sure, is popular, and so is its companion Lyft. Netflix has an app. You can use one with your bank and check your stocks on one. Oh, and Twitter for sure. You navigate with an app. How did you ever get anywhere without it?

Subway wants you on its app, and so do McDonald's, Wendy's, and Burger King. You likely read your news on an app and your sports on the ESPN app. or the Bleacher Report app. Order your hamburger on an app and get it delivered from an app. You use apps even when you don't know you're doing it.

So, for meditation, load in the app, and you're about done with the question of when and where and how to meditate. Play your app, sit back, and enjoy. It's time to reach for the trending, surely-this-works solution. Nothing, maybe not even yoga, is more the go-to place for worriers than meditation apps on the phone. They're so great. Flip them on when you need a little comfort. Flip them off when you have to go into a meeting or focus on your kid who's asking you to play a little Candyland.

- Insight Timer

- Yoga Glo

- Headspace (What a great name, not that all of these don't have great names. "Headspace," right? Love it.)

- Enso meditation by Salubrion (And there's another great name. "Salubrion." A million-dollar name.)

- Waking Up with Sam Harris – Unlock your mind

Wait, there's more in this top ten list I got off the Web.

- Ten Percent Happier (for the aim-low, undemanding worriers, I guess. Any relief is good.)

- Calm (Check this out. According to a report from "Entrepreneur" online Calm went "from $0 to $1 Billion Valuation in 7 Years." Stagger me. Are you kidding? Holy smokes. A practice with that kind of numbers has gotta help anxiety.)

Hey, when the going gets tough, go with the trendiest, and you can do it with that electronic device in your pocket. Wondering how to stop worrying and start living in the 21st? Pull out your phone and click here. Or, getting truly down to the nitty gritty, click a button for whatever effect you want.

"Meditate. Sleep. Relax." Calm offers that at the outset. Load it in. Choose from the icons. "Calming Anxiety." That's why we're here. Try that. You can do it for ten minutes. "Body Scan" is five minutes. "Deep Sleep" is five minutes. 'Daily Calm Highlights Resilience" is ten minutes.

The anxiety one, and almost all of the ones for learning to relax, are guided meditations. A calm, soothing voice comes on. "Start by finding a position that is comfortable. Find a position that is comfortable with a straight, relaxed back."

You follow the instructions, and you relax. How do you choose from among Calm and Insight Timer and Yoga Glo? It's a shopping choice. Compare prices. See if you like the sound of one or another. Look on Yelp. The app will almost certainly relax you. That should be good enough, and, obviously, for many, many people that is good enough. If it helps you sleep, oh, my. How precious is that. Switch it on. Click on the Sleep icon. Enter dreamland.

Failure to Launch

Am I going to find fault here? Yes, I guess so. We need a comparison between these apps, which do guided meditations, and the Transcendental Meditation® technique, which is not a guided meditation but a dive inside. These sweet and relaxing apps do not really go inside. Like those promising but so disappointing self-help books, the apps do not get beyond the level of our thinking. The brain waves in listening to a guided meditation are equivalent to those in daydreaming. Daydreaming is great, don't get me wrong. Isn't that what we do in the shower? What more creative place on earth is there than the bathtub and shower?

What I'm saying, to be clear, is that these apps are not the seemingly "impossible" fix that we're talking about achieving here. Nothing wrong with not being this. A popsicle is not doing anything wrong by not being Ben and Jerry's Cherry Garcia ice cream. But it is not that creamy, top-shelf ice cream. It is just water with flavoring.

As for listening to an app, it is just a temporary escape from our stress. The worry is still there or, to be more precise, the stress is still there. We don't dislodge it. We escape it for a few minutes maybe. Then it strikes again. That calming effect is not truly awesome. It's nice. That's all. It doesn't give us the power of amazing possibilities.

These apps are not effortless. Wait. They aren't? How much effort does it take to listen to an app and drift into your own daydreaming? It takes a little effort to concentrate. Know what else? The voice keeps interrupting your reverie. I find that a little bit annoying.

Daydreaming, not having any real purpose and not accomplishing any focused work, is a waste of time really except that the break in the action is good, like a palate-clearing sherbet in a big meal. It's not real work on your stress is all I'm saying. And for me, it's a waste of time.

The TM® Digital Course (App)

The classic Transcendental Meditation® program itself now has its own digital course that you play on your phone, so we can't speak of all the other apps as simply "those meditation apps." I don't think it was developed in response to all those other successful apps. Certainly they may have planted the idea. The app for the TM® technique has one fundamental difference from the other apps. You do not do your first day on your phone. You do the training in person with a certified teacher who gives you an experience that is deeper and more fundamental than happens with a guided meditation. You get the experience of transcending.

The digital course for the TM® program has a second difference, too. It does not offer guided meditations. You don't play the app to give you the experience of meditating. But the digital course is a nice way to give further instruction on the technique once you have learned it in person on the first day.

Third, while we're talking about these things, you are still involved with a certified teacher and with the formal organization for the TM® program as you go along and do the daily practice of the Transcendental Meditation® technique on your own (not guided by an app) for the rest of your life. That certified teacher you learn from in person is not just answering questions. He or she is assuring that you have the experience that is not daydreaming but is transcending.

All right, here's a fourth thing. The meditating that you do with the digital course for the TM® technique is completely effortless. No strain. None. It's simple and smooth. There's a reversing of "impossible" for you to think about. The specialty of the certified instructor for the TM® program is offering genuine effortlessness, and the teacher has had months of training to learn how to give you this experience and the ongoing follow-up training.

The other apps, too, don't have the hundreds of scientific research studies showing their effectiveness that the Transcendental Meditation® program has. Many of them are offering mindfulness practices, and mindfulness is often an academic field (Cognitive Behavioral Therapy) with its own burden of research. Comparing those researches is a bit of a "who shot John." You have to hope that they have the data to back up their statements like this in a Headspace ad: "Get 16% Happier in Just 10 Days."

I don't think that Headspace and Calm and Yoga Glo really see themselves in the marketspace occupied by candidates with serious depression, panic attacks, and any of those major, almost unfixable conditions that were bringing people to an introductory lecture on the Transcendental Meditation® program. Nor do teachers of the TM® program represent ourselves as providing medical treatments. The TM® technique is a light and lively way to use more and more of your mental potential and get the benefits of lowering blood pressure and help with stress. But we offer it in almost an offhanded way. "Try it if you want."

But those visitors I described in the opening chapter are looking for something more than a Band-Aid. They don't, for the most part, want to have an idle reverie for a few minutes. They want to be rescued. Chances are they have already tried one of the other apps besides the digital course in the TM® program. They have come to the TM® program, the great granddaddy of meditation techniques, the one recommended by Seinfeld and Howard Stern and a who's who of celebrities because they want something deep and powerful. In many cases, they want it all. They don't like paying for it. These apps don't cost much, and you can try them for free. But those coming hat-in-hand to the TM® program are ready, reluctantly, even to shell out a few shekels if they can just find some relief. Please, God, some relief. Get serious about your meditation. Often their first step is to learn a meditation they can learn from a book or from a friend or at least learn for less money than the TM® technique. They think about learning Mindfulness.

Chapter 7

Be Mindful: "Just Live in The Now."

"Since meeting with Jim and learning TM® I feel a reduction of stress and anxiety, which is saying a lot in this time of the COVID-19 scare. I have done many meditations, and I feel that TM® really reaches the essence of what meditation is."

PAUL VARGAS
Keyboarder for the popular eighties band Missing Persons

There's gotta be some way out of all this worry, but know what? Maybe not. "I have measured out my life with coffee spoons," says the obviously miserable J. Alfred Prufrock in the poem by T.S. Eliot, sounding much like those people in the introductory talks who feel full on the outside and empty on the inside. You can solve almost anything else. You can feed yourself and your kids, shelter yourself in grand style, and get a Mercedes. Then, royally fed, you can sit inside your palatial house on the hill and worry about the rats in the yard that aren't actually there or "Maybe a mountain lion will attack my grandson. I think I hear one now. Coyotes will attack a small child, and they travel in packs. The kid can be gone before you get to him, as if attacked by piranhas." You can get everything right except for the worrying. Nothing seems to work for that.

Time to continue the never-ending quest for relief. How about trying meditation? Mindfulness meditation. That's the one everybody does. It must be good with so many adherents. It's worth a shot, and no harm done if it doesn't work. Whatever, right? Mindfulness does have certain benefits. As Dr. Tony Nader asserts in his book *One Unbounded Ocean of Consciousness*, "People do experience benefits and relaxation from various mindfulness approaches. Mindfulness techniques can also momentarily divert the attention from stress and help to create a more favorable mental state for a richer experience."

Dead Man Walking

One question, often overlooked, is "Could mindfulness actually be harmful?" That is the forbidden question. It is forbidden by mindfulness people themselves, I imagine, mainly because they would never even think it in the first place. The movement teaching the Transcendental Meditation® program, for its part, takes the high road. It is a breach of etiquette to speak ill of another system.

So the question remains unasked. Why would I or anyone be contemplating even the possibility that such a heralded practice might be less than beneficial or, to be precise, even harmful? Well, there is one fellow I met who might. He is a genuine seeker of the most sincere sort. Where others might end their pursuit of self-development, he was only beginning. Many have the desire to quiet the mind. His desire was to silence the mind altogether . . . to stop thinking. And he had convinced himself that he had succeeded. He had suppressed his thinking, using mindfulness practices. There was a flatness to his visage. The man was stifled. Stuffing his thoughts had turned him, in my estimation, into somewhat of a dead man walking. Further, he was, in my perception, a capped volcano, and therein he was even dangerous. Do not uncap the volcano in this "peaceful," "unruffled," "enlightened" man.

Fine, this is one example of why I think mindfulness might actually not be so good. Another example, also anecdotal, is a man I met at a concert in the Berkshires a few years back. Socially, the man simply was not good company. He was fun at first, before he remembered and implemented his practice of being aware of himself while he was doing other things. Before that, he had good quips and ready enough conversation (I mean, nothing world-shaking, but he was a person and answered questions).

Then when he amped up his mindfulness, he disconnected from us. His attention went to himself, and he was a bit too certain about how important this was. He seemed to know something the rest of us did not. He was living in the moment, and it certainly seemed those in his presence were not in that moment. He himself was the moment he sought. I don't mean to be unkind. I'm sorry. But he could have been laughing and casting meaningless, clever asides along with the rest of us. Instead he was riveted onto himself. I don't know. I missed being with him. What was so important that he had to lie there just to keep his attention on himself?

In his book *One Unbounded Ocean of Consciousness,* Dr. Nader explains how mindfulness practices might sometimes be harmful. "Attempting to be mindful during daily activity can divide the attention between the action and the mental pressure required to be mindful while completing the action. . . . Trying to be mindful in this way can lead to anxiety and performance inefficiency, especially when mindfulness becomes an artificial mood rather than a genuine experience."

Gosh, a lot of the time I just don't know what to say to people when they say they've been "meditating" for maybe twenty years by practicing mindfulness. I have to wonder where they got that much stamina and grit, qualities that at least one mindfulness site says you should have to succeed with the practice. And I have to wonder, though you would never say it to them, that same unaskable and completely inappropriate question: Was it even good for them? Had they been, in all their ardor and passion, wasting their time and not doing much for themselves? The concern about them is kind of the elephant in the room when you're talking with a mindfulness person, especially a dedicated one. You did all that work. Could it have been harmful?

And how does mindfulness lessen your anxiety? That's another embarrassing one in a conversation. I mean, what is a practice of "being mindful" doing to chill you out? Yes, mindfulness is used in their practice by lots of cognitive behavioral psychologists and, well, it's everywhere. You can't pop into a yoga class without having people talk about "being in the now." You might even get that at the bank or standing in line at a movie theater—the "being in the now." But being in the now might not mean you're not anxious. You might just tune in to your anxiety or have the anxiety as kind of an invisible partner while you read the posters on the wall of the movie theater.

Or, to be fair, mindfulness may take your mind off your worries. Your worries are from instances in the past or from possible mischances that can happen in the future. If your awareness is on neither the past nor the future, you can have no fodder for worry. I suppose it can work. But is it fundamental? Is it rooting out the worry, or is the worry just waiting until you are too tired to be carefully fixing your attention on the moment? Mindfulness is a form of thinking, not a way of moving from the surface level of the mind to deeper levels. The TM® technique is the one practice to do that by moving within, as Figure 7.1 shows.

Thoughts rise in the mind like bubbles from the floor of the ocean. Other practices experience thoughts on the surface. The TM® technique takes us beneath the surface.

The table comparing stress markers in TM® and mindfulness shows the same difference, flatly stated. The TM® technique has been shown to reduce stress markers like cortisol and faster breathing; mindfulness does not.

It's easy to see some of why practicing mindfulness is so widespread. Meditation is in the air, so people want to do it. With the TM® technique, you have to learn the practice from a trained instructor. This is not really so with mindfulness. You can have a friend teach you, who reads an article about it in a magazine. You can just start doing it or perhaps watch a video on YouTube to get you launched.

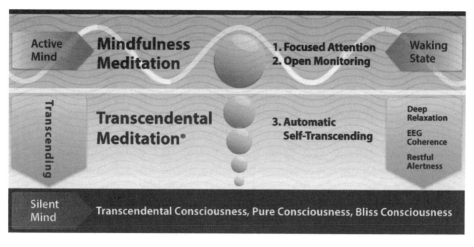

Reference: *Consciousness and Cognition* 19, no. 4 (2010): 1110–1118.

Figure 7.1 Thoughts rise in the mind like bubbles from the floor of the ocean. Mindfulness meditation happens on the surface. Transcending goes to the depths.

TM reduces physiological stress markers.
Mindfulness does not.

Transcendental Meditation	Mindfulness Meditation
When the mind settles down during TM, the corresponding physiological changes are just the opposite of the stress response.	Focused Attention and Open Monitoring keep the mind on active thinking, and the physiology does not settle down.

Reference: *Consciousness and Cognition* 19, no. 4 (2010): 1110–1118.

And what do you experience? Here's a description I found from "Greater Good Magazine":

> "Mindfulness means maintaining a moment-by-moment awareness of our thoughts, feelings, bodily sensations, and surrounding environment, through a gentle, nurturing lens. . . . When we practice mindfulness, our thoughts tune into what we're sensing in the present moment rather than rehashing the past or imagining the future."
>
> —"Greater Good Magazine"
> The Greater Good Science Center at the
> University of California, Berkeley

I'm just wondering, not to be difficult or anything, how you can be aware of all those things (thoughts, feeling, bodily sensations, and surrounding environment). Do you riff through them one at a time? Choose one? Just be open and see what comes up? (It's probably this one.)

Grit, Determination, and Discipline

When people meditate with mindfulness, they often tell me they're not really sure if they're doing it, meaning meditating. Now, the thing is, even its exponents say it's hard to do.

As the Buddhist monk Bhante Henepola Gunaratana says in his popular book *Mindfulness in Plain English*: "Meditation is not easy. It takes time and it takes energy. It also takes grit, determination, and discipline. We can sum it all up in the American word 'gumption.' Meditation takes gumption."

Does effort like this make us less anxious? Sure, I guess it could. Maybe it does for some people.

Figure 7.2 shows data of a study comparing the TM® technique with other practices. Note that one concentration practice (and mindfulness is sometimes a concentration practice) actually increases anxiety.

The TM® technique is twice as effective as everything else. Having a placebo sounds great. We all love a placebo, which somehow gets our Freudian subconscious to kick in. In this case the placebo, in spite of its fancy name, is simply sitting with your eyes closed. Doing the non-TM® meditation practices in this study had the same effect as sitting with the

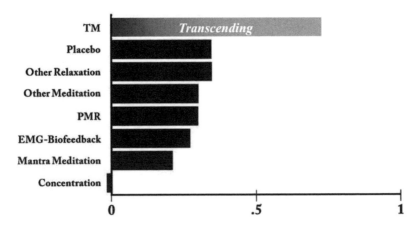

Transcending vs. Relaxation
Effectiveness in Reducing Trait Anxiety
Meta-Analysis 146 studies

Reference: *Journal of Clinical Psychology* 45, no. 6 (1989): 957–74.

Figure 7.2 The TM® technique reduces trait anxiety (stress) twice as much as other practices, including the "placebo," which is sitting with the eyes closed.

eyes closed. Well, just sitting with your eyes shut is boring. It's certainly not fun. We miss out on whatever is going on around us. It is hardly any self-revolutionizing practice. (And, oh, someone silence me—it makes us a little bit dull, maybe.)

There is important research comparing mindfulness with the TM® technique for anxiety. Figure 7.3 shows the TM® technique was more effective than Mindfulness for reducing anxiety.

The study concluded that the TM® technique reduces anxiety more than mindfulness, but I don't know; that's not really all that definitive. Mindfulness in such studies has some effect, but it is again the same effect as sitting with the eyes closed—hardly a powerhouse in anxiety relief, and most of us can sit with our eyes closed doing nothing for about a nanosecond, at best, if we're awake.

Nor is another study that looked at the TM® technique for post-traumatic stress a great source for showing a dramatic difference

Comparison of TM and Mindfulness on Anxiety Reduction

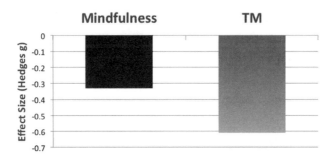

TM decreases anxiety more than mindfulness meditation

References: *Journal of Alternative and Complementary Medicine* 19 (2013): 1–12; *Journal of Consulting Clinical Psychology* 78(2) (2010): 169–183.

Figure 7.3 The TM® technique reduces anxiety more than mindfulness.

between the TM® technique and mindfulness. But it shows a difference and cites studies in a number of reliable journals from 2011 back to 1985, including the *Journal of Counseling and Development*. The numerous studies were all able to replicate the result, so that, yes, they indicated the TM® technique reduces stress more effectively than mindfulness.

The science kind of bends over backward to be fair because it seems to me that often the rub with mindfulness is that it just plain doesn't work. It's frustrating—not really doing much for anxiety and sometimes even increasing it.

Mindfulness is summed up in the table "Physiological Effects in a Nutshell." The TM® technique gets rid of the enemy, which is stress. Mindfulness doesn't actually do that. The TM® technique, as we settle into a relaxed (and for some people "euphoric") state, shows up as alpha EEG coherence. Mindfulness doesn't.

"I Just Did It When I Was in Class"

Arlo, a songwriter, had a mindfulness class in college—UCLA, I think. "I just did it when I was in class." What about doing it at home? "I'd just go do something else," he reports. "It was way too confusing, with too many moving parts. And we'd learn a different one every week." This sounds nicely academic but hardly something helpful to remove stress. In fact, in my experience most things that are academic don't relieve stress. They pile it on.

Physiological Effects in a Nutshell

Transcendental Meditation	Mindfulness Meditation
The physiological effects of TM are the opposite of stress, and it increases alpha EEG coherence.	Mindfulness practices do not reduce stress markers, and they have no effect on alpha EEG coherence.

References: *Consciousness and Cognition* 19, no. 4 (2010): 1110–1118. *American Psychologist* 42 (1987): 879–881.

Another practitioner of the TM® technique told her experience with mindfulness. In her comparison between the TM® technique and mindfulness, she said, "I like the ease of it (the TM® technique). It feels really nice not to try." Feeling really nice is one kind of relief from anxiety. Not needing to "try" to meditate, in itself, doesn't really bring the relief. The transcending brings relief. But for Jackie, not trying in itself was a good start.

Here's what a young man named Jonas said about his experience of trying ways to practice meditation after he learned the TM® technique. "All these other ones were so hard and took so long to get anywhere. The TM® technique is so much deeper and faster." Sean, a mindfulness teacher in public schools, said when he learned the TM® technique: "I felt like I skipped a few steps." (And he felt he went straight to the goal.) Daniel, a lawyer who learned the TM® technique, gave his viewpoint. "I've been exposed to Buddhism a lot because I spent years and years in Asia, and so I've always been interested in it and tried various methods when I was younger, and I failed in my eyes—and my own mind." (Vipassana, a Buddhist practice, is a form of mindfulness or, rather, the other way around.) With the TM® technique he felt he finally succeeded.

Buddhist monks all over the world, especially in Asia, do concentration practices like Vipassana. They are well-known for doing these sessions for two hours at a stretch and often much longer. Sometimes people go on retreats where they meditate for days. I've heard people tell about doing concentration practices for four days. They sometimes mention their profound experiences, like the person who told me she had the same experience in her first few minutes of the TM® technique that she had near the end of one of the multi-day retreats she attended. When a monk was discussing his long sessions with a friend of mine who practices the TM® technique he asked my friend, "What do you do about the headaches?" Concentrating can be a bit of a strain on the old noggin.

Let's take that thing of being "present," too. How did they put it? They said it meant: "Maintaining a moment-by-moment awareness of our thoughts, feelings, bodily sensations, and surrounding environment through a gentle, nurturing lens." You know what? It seems to me that you can't really do that. Nobody can really do it, whether the lens is gentle and nurturing or not. All this verbiage about being present doesn't seem to have much of a deliverable.

Here's a statement from a mindfulness website called Mind and Movement:

> "Mindfulness is a quality of human consciousness character-ized by an accepting awareness of and enhanced attention to the constant stream of lived experience. Being mindful increases engagement with the present moment and allows for a clearer understanding of how thoughts and emotions can impact our health and quality of life."

This can lead one to wonder, "Is this anything that I'd really want to pursue? Sounds complicated and maybe a bit weird." Please forgive my bluntness. I just picture myself when I was seeking, before I came to learn the TM® technique and remember how I would have felt if presented with such verbiage. Not pretty to think about. At that time I could get nasty. Also, apparently, and importantly, gaining what they call "a clearer understanding" does not have such an immediate and measurable effect on health. The American Heart Association (AHA), as you can see in figure 7.4, was frank about it when they advised doctors that they could recommend the TM® technique for high blood pressure but not MBSR (Mindfulness Based Stress Reduction).

It just flat-out didn't recommend mindfulness meditation by name. You can be polite and say that the practice of mindfulness just didn't have the research to validate that it had much effect. Yes, let's be polite here. But the question remains. Perhaps mindfulness doesn't have much research backing it. Maybe it does not have the desired effect.

So, sure, mindfulness is the most well-known form of meditation, and the Transcendental Meditation® technique is this solid, trudg-ing-ahead practice that people come to only when they're desperate and have exhausted other possibilities that often include mindfulness. The lingo from mindfulness practice has entered the mainstream. You can tell who's been catching the ongoing talk about personal growth

American Heart Association

". . . the Transcendental Meditation technique is the only meditation practice that has been shown to lower blood pressure . . . all other meditation techniques (including MBSR [Mindfulness Based Stress Reduction]) received a 'Class III, no benefit, Level of Evidence C' recommendation and are not recommended in clinical practice to lower blood pressure at this time."

Reference: *Hypertension: Journal of the American Heart Association,* no. 61 (2013): 6.

Figure 7.4 American Heart Association statement on the TM® technique and blood pressure.[1] Figure taken from standard Maharishi Foundation USA materials.

when he or she talks about "being in the moment," but even guy-on-the-street regular people talk about "being mindful." "Meditation" to almost everybody means sitting with your back straight and focusing on your breath, as is common in some forms of mindfulness (in fact, most forms).

Mindfulness meditation has succeeded the most in terms of popularity, recognizability, and penetration of meditation into the mainstream. But judging from the people who come to us for the TM® technique, I suspect maybe it just really doesn't do enough for anxiety. Thinking again of our unhappy searching people from that initial meeting, I have to think about how I would feel if I were also offering just one more version of concentrating on the present instead of offering, as I am, a means to dive deep inside.

But on the other hand, I did meet a nurse the other day who has been practicing mindfulness meditation and said, "It works, and it helped me a lot." She had come in to learn the TM® technique, but nevertheless we can't make too much of that. I don't even remember if she actually started the program.

Mindfulness meditation obviously must do some good. "It's good for the things it's good for," a scientist in the program told me, having heard about the blowback I received from a mindfulness writer in Hong Kong. Most of the mindfulness people never come our way, and we don't get to teach them the TM® technique. A few do, of course. And sometimes they're beside themselves with gratitude with the results that come from transcending as opposed to simply being in the moment.

I know it seems impolite and perhaps a bit roguish to suggest that mindfulness can be anything worse than a harmless habit that is good only for some people. Perhaps we should leave it at that, but of course I haven't just left it at that. I've raised the unaskable question: "Might it even be harmful to close the eyes and concentrate a lot on the present moment?" I suppose I shouldn't have brought this up. After all, we live in a civil society and want to uplift one another.

Sometimes, though, I think we ought to warn people, or at least try to reinforce their perception, that certain practices aren't just happy fads. They can be harmful. Some practices might not be just a waste of time and a little frustrating. It is a shame, too, for people to rule out something called "meditating" because of an unfortunate experience with a concentration technique that made them decide maybe this stuff just doesn't work for them. On the other hand, if you dedicate yourself to concentration approaches with all the zeal of a genuine seeker, you might . . . oh, well, maybe I've already said enough about the risks . . . but to finish this thought: You should be aware that with a wrong approach you might shut down your thinking a bit too much—or even a lot too much.

Sometimes people seeking relaxation are confused about their meditation experience and want to cut straight to the chase to eliminate uncertainty and ambivalence. They might think they are just having a fleeting mood change when "living in the moment"—or what's happening to them isn't quite real. They begin to look for another source of tranquility and end up asking for a prescription. They start taking pills.

CHAPTER 8

Pop This Pill. Oh, and That One, Too.

"According to a government study, antidepressants have become the most commonly prescribed drugs in the United States. They're prescribed more than drugs to treat high blood pressure, high cholesterol, asthma, or headaches."

"CDC: Antidepressants most prescribed drugs in U.S." CNN.com

Pills control the relaxation marketplace, for sure. They come backed by the authority of modern medicine. Upset? Pop a pill. Some people, a physician was explaining to me recently, may take two or three sedatives. You smooth over. Pop a pill, and head into that meeting. There you are with chill in a pill.

Look to get exact statistics on Xanax or Lexapro prescriptions, and you may feel overwhelmed and confused. Look for the most recent statistics, and the problem gets even more challenging. An article on the website Forbes.com by Matthew Herper stated, "Doctors write nearly 50 million prescriptions for Xanax or alprazolam (the cheap, generic equivalent) every year—that's more than one Xanax prescription every second." That was in 2010. According to the website ClinCalc.com, prescriptions for another popular sedative, Escitalopram (the generic form of Lexapro) were 27,510,958. Other sources state that the pandemic and outbreaks of war have further increased the numbers. One thing is certain. The number of antidepressants prescribed is really high.

I don't think the number is nearly so high for people practicing the TM® technique. Sure, these medications dominate the relief-from-anxiety marketplace. But that doesn't stop some people from trickling over to the TM® technique, the all-natural solution that also promises relief from worry, anxiety, depression, and stress in its myriad forms.

Serotonin, the Great Relaxer

Now, first of all, both of them work. Take a pill, and you relax. Do your TM® technique, and you relax. As far as calming down and finding some tranquility and repose is concerned, they both work in the same way. Lexapro, that is, is an SSRI, which is a phrase lots of us love to say: "selective serotonin reuptake inhibitor." Nice. It prevents the body from taking back the serotonin it has put into the bloodstream, thereby increasing serotonin. Serotonin itself is a neurotransmitter that does things to make us feel good. According to a graduate student's dissertation I came across on this subject, the TM® technique increases serotonin, too. Or, as the PhD candidate put it, "The highly significant increase of 5-HIAA (5-hydroxyindole-3-acetic acid) in the Transcendental Meditation® technique suggests systemic serotonin as 'rest and fulfillment hormone' of deactivation-relaxation."*

Surely you'd think that the tranquilizer would work faster and deeper than the TM® technique, but the TM® technique may be much more fast-acting than the sedatives. According to the website www.anxieties.com, "It takes four to six weeks to notice significant therapeutic benefits from the SSRIs. The full range of benefits can take twelve weeks." People begin noticing benefits from the TM® technique right away. The site notes a few other effects of tranquilizers that might give you pause. "Patients often experience a temporary worsening of anxiety symptoms during the first two weeks of treatment. Abrupt discontinuation of the SSRIs could cause flu-like symptoms. All the SSRIs can be expensive."

Sedatives—No Cumulative Benefits

All you're trying to do is take a pill, a prescription pill straight from your trusted family doc, and get some relief. You get it, but think about the comparison with the natural, eyes-closed, no-effort practice of the TM® technique.

The benefit ends when the effect of the drug wears off. For instance, you take a Lexapro once a day. Then you take it again the next day, and so on, with no real end in sight. You're still anxious at your baseline,

---

*Relationship between subjective bliss, 5-hydroxy-3-indoleacetic acid and the collective practice of Maharishi's Transcendental Meditation® and the TM® -Sidhi program, dissertation by Sarah-Annelies Loliger.

but you do feel better for a day. With the TM® technique, interestingly, the full benefits also mostly wear off within 24 hours, but some of its smoothing effects continue. The benefits actually accrue, like your bank savings, an appropriate comparison if you are one of the rare people who has a savings account. You do have to do another meditation with the TM® technique to continue to accrue the relief you feel. But to some degree, maybe to a very small degree if you didn't meditate for many days or weeks, you receive a benefit simply from having started practicing the TM® technique.

The pills are going to cost you about $100 a month. ("What? Really so much?") At the beginning, depending on the deal you work out when you decide to learn the TM® technique, the cost of the pills is usually less than your meditation. However, the TM® program is a one-time cost that covers you for life. You pay every month for your pills. After a few months, the escitalopram (Lexapro) will continue to hit you for the $100 a month, soon surpassing the cost of the TM® with no end in sight. Now wait, this is hardly definitive for deciding your choice. There's much more to consider.

It is not recommended to mix Lexapro with alcohol. A website site called www.medicalnewstoday.com gives this information: "People who drink alcohol while taking Lexapro may feel more depressed or anxious, and these symptoms may then become more challenging to treat. . . . Drinking alcohol may also worsen some of the side effects of Lexapro or other antidepressants, including drowsiness and dizziness." Not a dealbreaker either, really, but the effects of drinking alcohol are not enhanced during your meditation. Just as drinking alcohol affects your mental state, the drinking can affect the meditation, but not vice versa. In fact in my experience, the meditation makes the effects of the drinking wear off a bit.

Side effects. Now we're getting into what people often worry about. According to Forest Pharmaceuticals, manufacturer of the drug Lexapro, taking it can cause the following reactions:

> Adverse events occurring in 2 percent or more of patients treated with Lexapro: dry mouth, sweating; headache, paresthesia; nausea, diarrhea, constipation, indigestion,

vomiting, abdominal pain, flatulence, toothache; fatigue, influenza-like symptoms; neck/shoulder pain; somnolence, insomnia, libido decreased, dreaming abnormal, appetite decreased, lethargy, yawning; ejaculation disorder, anorgasmia, menstrual disorder.

This is quite a list. I have no clue what paresthesia is, but I'll look it up for you. Okay, I see it's the feeling of prickling in the arms or legs or wherever. I do know what the other things mentioned are. Like "flatulence." Sure don't want that.

Most people will have few or none of these reactions. That's not the point. People hate taking pills. They don't necessarily read through the long list of side effects. They usually don't know which effects they might experience and which they are unlikely to encounter. They just, really, really don't want to risk having any of those things. They don't like putting something weird in their bodies. So, yes, the many potential side effects can be a deal breaker.

Here is a table showing an admittedly TM® technique-slanted comparison of the side effects of sedatives and the (in quotation marks) "side effects" of the TM® technique (because the TM® technique has only good side effects).

Some people don't like that an SSRI doesn't really treat the underlying problem but only masks it. "Basically, it just, like, numbs your brain. You can't get much work done either," says Donna, a successful businesswoman who opted for the TM® technique as a way out of depression. Phoebe, a nurse, protests that she's reached her limit of taking an SSRI. "Basically, it makes me more normal. It doesn't make me happy. It doesn't make me better." Never actually getting better from a category of drugs is quite a knock on a product. But millions of prescriptions are filled for them because people are willing to go ahead with sedating antidepressants whether they are a long-term solution or not.

The unmentionable side effect, completely one-sided and unfair—is suicide. That's the skeleton in the closet with these sedatives. Suicide is the unthinkable solution. But we have to go there a little bit. A website called www.bmj.com as well as a host of others states the following: "Antidepressants increase the risk of suicide, violence, and homicide at all ages." Yikes, homicide, too. We're playing with firearms here when actually we're just trying to make a point of comparison and move on. We don't mean to use scare tactics or anything. That's not like us. But you do need to have "suicide risk" somewhere on your checklist when thinking about taking an SSRI or other kinds of antidepressants.

The TM® technique, on the other hand, by all accounts of the people I've known, is suicide preventive. People become happier and less prone to self-destruction. Of course, there have been occasional suicides among those who practice the TM® technique, as there are in any demographic. But I've heard many veterans talk about how the TM® technique took away their suicidal tendencies.

The TM® Technique—Effective, Non-Addictive, and Free

Nobody is going to say that the TM® technique will take over the anti-anxiety marketplace and replace, SSRI's, tranquilizers, and "xannies." The relief from sedatives is immediate (okay, after a little wait to get used to them), they're really cheap (What's three dollars a day to someone who's miserable?), they get you feeling better (maybe even get you high), and they come with the blessing of your doctor. They're rolling all over the counter in homes around the world. "Take a valium like a normal person," shouts one disgruntled person in the movie *Desperately Seeking Susan* from the 1980s. Maybe now it would have to be "take a Xanax already," but you know what I mean.

Still, the TM® technique is a fascinating possible alternative for those in the know. It chills you out, man. It's basically free. It doesn't give you the shakes or make you throw up or pass gas or any of the side effects the manufacturers admit to on the back of the pill box (that, in fairness, don't usually happen but might). The risk of addiction raises its ugly head, too, and the TM® technique is not addictive. Truly. The TM® technique increases serotonin in the body but does not cause a spike of dopamine (known for its link to addiction) in the brain. At any rate, people in great crisis don't stop to think about the risk of addiction. It's just "You mean I can get some relief? Please give me some!"

Side Effects of Anxiety Medication*	"Side Effects" of Transcendental Meditation
Drowsiness, lack of energy	Restful alertness (1, 2)
Clumsiness, slow reflexes	Faster reactions (3)
Slurred speech	Improved speech (4)
Confusion and disorientation	Increased field independence (3)
Depression	Decreased depression (5)
Dizziness, lightheadedness	Increased presence oriented (6)
Impaired thinking and judgment	Increased intelligence and creativity (3)
Memory loss, forgetfulness	Improved memory (7)
Nausea, stomach upset	Decreased gastrointestinal disorders (8)
Blurred or double vision	Improved visual perception (9)

*Benzodiazepines or tranquilizers. "Anxiety Medications."
http://www.helpguide.org/articles/anxiety/anxietymedication.htm.

Here are the journal articles about "side effects" of the TM® technique referenced by the numbers in parentheses in the table:

1. Wallace, R.K., "Physiological Effects of Transcendental Meditation," *Science* (1970).
2. Wallace, R.K., Benson, H., Wilson, A.F. "A Wakeful Hypometabolic Physiologic State," *American Journal of Physiology* (1971).
3. So, K.T., Orme-Johnson, D.W. "Three Randomized Experiments on the Holistic Longitudinal Effects of the Transcendental Meditation Technique on Cognition," *Intelligence* (2001).
4. Everman, J. "Transcendental Meditation and Mental Retardation," *Journal of Clinical Psychiatry* (1981).
5. Sheppard, W.D., Staggers, F., Johns, L. "The Effects of a Stress Management Program in a High Security Government Agency," *Anxiety, Stress, and Coping* (1997).
6. Alexander, C.N., Rainforth, M.V., Gelderloos, P. "Transcendental Meditation, Self-Actualization and Psychological Health: A Conceptual Overview and Statistical Meta-Analysis," *Journal of Social Behavior and Personality* (1991).
7. Alexander, C.N., Barnes, V.A., Schneider, R.H., Langer, E.J., Newman, R.I., Chandler, H.M., et al. "A Randomized Controlled Trial of Stress Reduction on Cardiovascular and All-Cause Mortality in the Elderly: Results of 8- and 15-Year Follow-Ups," *Circulation* (1996).
8. Orme-Johnson, D.W., "Medical Care Utilization and the Transcendental Meditation Program," *Psychosomatic Medicine* (1987).
9. Dillbeck, M.C. "The Effect of Transcendental Meditation on Anxiety Level," *Journal of Clinical Psychology* (1977).

What other stops do people make before resorting to the famous TM® technique? A popular place for people to go is the practice that costs money for most people in America most of the time. It's the popular treatment of psychotherapy that used to have a bad name, but I'm going way back to say that, like to the fifties. Nowadays therapy is as commonplace as YouTube or Amazon Prime. A fascinating study funded by your US Government compared the TM® technique and therapy. People go to therapy, for sure, and they expect it to cost money. Is therapy the seemingly impossible solution for stress and anxiety? It's more likely the fallback solution and may get you some pills, too.

CHAPTER 9

Please lie down on the couch.

"Prior to the TM® technique I had tried many forms of meditation, but I suppose, in part due to my ADD, none of them proved effective. If you are suffering (as I was) with depression please consider the TM® technique as part of your therapy, for me it has turned out to be the mainstay of my therapy, and I must note that I do not take any depression medications. I would like to thank Jim and Nina for being such wonderful guides."

Sincerely, Joseph

It's not just the people who have passed through my lecture hall who speak of hopelessness, futility, and fear, of course. It's all kinds of people coming to learn the TM® technique all over the world. Seriously. When I taught the TM® technique to Maasai people in Tanzania, the story was the same. "I'm worried about the crops," and, boy, that was a lot to worry about. They'd have a plot about the size of an ordinary back yard, and they'd have to live year-round from what came out of it. No wonder they were worried. Nevertheless, after practicing the TM® technique they often said, "I feel better."

Exposure Therapy. Déjà vu All Over Again

Perhaps nowhere do the stark contrasts between the TM® technique and psychotherapy show up more completely than with Post-Traumatic Stress Disorder (PTSD) Veterans. I did meet such veterans myself when working with the Wounded Warrior Battalion at Camp Pendleton North of San Diego. When I taught them, they were a polite and cooperative group, to be sure. I taught the men, and my wife taught the women. They had seen more than most of the rest of us have to see and of course showed signs of it.

I was there when some of their leaders offered an outing to a Lakers' game to anyone interested. Kobe was in his heyday. These were choice tickets. My hands were twitching a little, wanting to seize a couple tickets. (In fairness, the Lakers weren't truly a great team anymore.) But in the veterans' stressed-out condition, kind of numb to the world around them, they didn't want to go. Getting on the bus, wandering through the arena, buying a hot dog, being in the crowds— all of it sounded just like too much effort. They didn't want to bother. Their experiences seemed to have drained some of the life out of them.

They had been in facilities where mortars came raining down. U.S. Marine or not, you still are inside a mass of protoplasm (your body), and hurtling metal and debris can end your life. These survivors had gotten through it, but some of them had buddies who were not so lucky.

One female veteran came to one of her follow-up meetings after instruction in TM®, smiling and cordial as in the previous meetings, certainly not appearing to be a threatening person, and she mildly recounted the loss of her recent job. What had happened to end her job? She told us someone had come up behind her and touched her on the back when she wasn't looking. She spared us the details, but the perpetrator of that perfectly innocent act apparently was not spared. Picture, then, the boiling cauldron inside this female veteran. She was holding it in, holding it in, holding it in. But she had encountered the wrong stimulus, and out it came.

The standard treatment for these vets with PTSD was "prolonged exposure therapy." For the most part, people suffering from anxiety and depression (often diagnosed informally by themselves) at our meetings did not have the degree of anxiety of these formally diagnosed vets. If these suburban people with malaise went through "talk therapy," they may have experienced some form of exposure therapy or they may have experienced instead a less structured form of treatment. However, exposure therapy is a form of talk therapy, and the comparison between TM® and exposure therapy is useful for showing how treatment with the TM® technique compares with talk therapy.

In exposure therapy, the patient relives the experience that caused the trauma. "A mortar hit our location." "We were lost in Baghdad when I realized we were in trouble." "I was supposed to disarm the ordnance we had located." "As a sniper, I was used to the impersonal act of killing. But this time it was different." The patient lives through it and lives though it and lives through it again until eventually the effect of the trauma is less for them.

To me, not being a PTSD patient, it's analogous to the kind of things we all do—forcing ourselves to do what we're afraid of. Such as speaking to groups. Driving on an LA freeway like the 101. Calling to ask for a date with someone you think you don't have a chance with. Trying out for a movie part. Interviewing for an executive position. We dread something, but we force ourselves to walk through it. Maybe our exposure to difficult situations never becomes outright easy, but we somehow do it. In exposure therapy, people relive over and over the experiences they most want never to live through again. And this does work. They begin to be able to live with their memories. Their trauma, so numbing, so panicking, begins to quiet down.

Not Reliving the Horror

Here we are, the Transcendental Meditation® program, with the ultimate, all-time anxiety solution. It calms the mind. It calms the body. It's progressive, building up an inner immunity to stress. So, we decided, with the aid of funding from the Veterans Administration of the United States, to put to the test our thinking that the TM® technique would work just as well as the exposure therapy and—Sound the trumpets!—without making these dedicated soldiers relive the fear and horror they went through. The title of the study is "Non-Trauma-Focused Meditation Versus Exposure Therapy in Veterans with Post-Traumatic Stress Disorder: A Randomised Controlled Trial" by Nidich S, Mill PJ, Rainforth M, et al., published in 2018.

Here is how the authors of the study interpret the results in their notes that appeared beneath one version of a chart of their data. "Veterans with PTSD who practiced the Transcendental Meditation® technique showed significant reductions in PTSD symptoms comparable to veterans who utilized a gold standard prolonged exposure therapy, according to a new study published in 'The Lancet Psychiatry' journal, Nov 15, 2018. Both Transcendental Meditation® and exposure therapy treatments were significantly more effective than the PTSD health education control group."

The scientists comparing the TM® technique with the gold-standard approach of prolonged treatment with exposure therapy stated that the veterans' reduced symptoms from practicing TM® were

Decreased PTSD in Veterans Published in
The Lancet Psychiatry

Reduction in PTSD Symptoms and Depression:
Comparison of TM, Prolonged Exposure, and Health Education

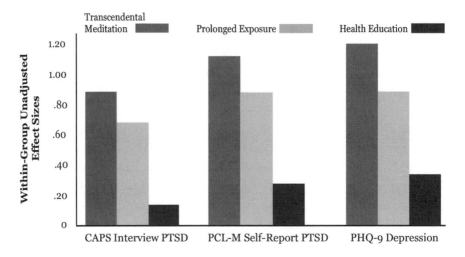

Effect Sizes: Small = .20   Medium = .50   Large = .80
Between-Group Comparisons Adjusted by ANCOVA:
TM vs. HE (p values < .001)   PE vs. HE (p values < .05)
TM vs. PE (p values < .001, non-inferiority comparisons)

Figure 9.1 The TM® technique lowers PTSD as well as the gold-standard psychiatric approach.[2]

"comparable," which is reasonable and does not, as it were, flaunt the results and perhaps cause a backlash. But this little-renowned living-room technique taught in a few short sessions over a few days, hung in there and might even have surpassed the "gold standard" treatment with a common-sense approach that just works away at the problem and moderates it.

Note, too, that the scientists compared the TM® technique not just with prolonged exposure therapy but also with "health education." This education is what we learn about the illness of PTSD from our doctors and the medical people and from texts about our condition— all coming from our intellect, from words alone without anything to transform us in our body. You can read about depression or anxiety or suicide risks. You can learn the background about the special challenges to the military in combat and the difficulties of transitioning to civilian life. You can read about alcoholism related to veterans. You'd think such information would help, but health education was a distant third behind the beneficial results from TM® technique and that gold standard of treatment (exposure therapy).

Nevertheless, most of those coming to the TM® technique to escape their stress do not have access to exposure therapy. They don't have the means. They don't have the time. And maybe they don't have the stomach to relive their own trauma, which may not be enough to earn them the official names of "PTSD" but is bad enough to send them into ongoing discomfort, sleep loss, and barely contained panic (okay, outright panic). One Vietnam vet that we taught more or less encapsulated this whole situation. He was 72 when we taught him the TM® technique. In his first day following instruction we asked him if he felt easy. "I have a volcano inside that is about to erupt," he answered.

That vet, a devoted patriot, had been a helicopter pilot in the Vietnam War, daring and treacherous work if ever there was. And as his teachers of the TM® technique, we didn't know what he had been through, and we didn't know if he remembered it, and we didn't ask him to relive it. That is, we did not use exposure therapy.

My wife took him into a separate room to give him a 10-minute session of special attention for his stress release before he did his regular meditation with the group. His few days of the TM® technique, with it's profound rest to the body, were giving his body an opportunity to clean out the built-up stresses in his system. She explained to him that thanks to his TM®, after more than 50 years of harboring that trauma, the stress was beginning to come out. His volcano was something good; it was the physical discharge of his pent-up tension. He returned to the room with a big grin on his face and a glow about him. Yes, here indeed was a therapy for post-traumatic stress.

Big Results Without Talk

The aforementioned notes in the scientists' chart refer to stories like those that every week pass through our center for teaching the TM® program: "The following are two excerpts of two 'patient perspectives' from veterans who were randomly assigned to learn the TM® technique," says the explanatory footnote to the chart. One 33-year-old man was in rough shape. He was diagnosed with depression and PTSD. The note said he had experienced "several" tours of duty in Iraq and Afghanistan. He couldn't sleep. He felt regret and uncertainty about his combat actions. Frighteningly, in the light of the high suicide rate among combat veterans, he said, "Sometimes I'd think I would be better off dead so that I didn't have to deal with it all." After beginning the TM® technique he began to sleep through the night. He felt better. He had more energy. His outlook about his future changed.

A woman from the study who had served in the Navy had "military sexual trauma" and PTSD. She was not the woman I mentioned who had the destructive episode with a woman who startled her, but she was in bad shape. She drank too much alcohol. She didn't want to leave her house. She wasn't driving anymore. After a few weeks of regular practice of the Transcendental Meditation® technique, she said, "I began to drive, and I started community college. TM® has given me my life back."

Psychotherapy is sacrosanct. It's such a standard part of our society that we continue it whether it's working or not. Sometimes it seems that almost everybody does it; it must be good for most people. However, it's not generally something that results in a fundamental change in our lives. It doesn't transform us. It doesn't leave us gasping in gratitude and appreciation. It may be what poet Robert Frost called "a momentary stay against confusion" in his essay "The Figure a Poem Makes." But we'll take it. Any port in a storm.

Many of those who come to us have been in therapy or are seeing a therapist. But it's not helpful enough. In some cases the therapist sends them to learn our practice, and the TM® becomes one more tool in their treatment. In any event, they want a lot of things. For starters, they want a solution to their anxiety. I'll tell you about some tormented Congo refugees who received exactly this from TM®.

PART III

The TM® Program

CHAPTER 10

Coping with Devastating Events

"The soldiers tortured me—almost killed me. Now, I feel like it happened to a different woman—not to me. I am a free woman."

ESPERANZA, A Congolese Refugee

You hear the rumors first. Soldiers have been raiding neighboring towns, and the horrors are unspeakable. You don't think this can happen to you. It is the 21st century. You live in a proper home, and you have a husband and children. You have a car. You think perhaps you should go to somewhere safe, but where would you go? And, anyway, you can't believe you'll be harmed.

When it does happen, you are so horrified that you become numb almost immediately. Young soldiers, like savages, burst onto your yard and into your house and wield their rifle butts with cruelty and abandon. They drag your husband, flailing and battling, into the back yard, and you hear the shots. It can't be true. They begin to assault you, and you lose consciousness.

Imagine such events occurring, as they did in the Congo to a group of women who later became refugees in Uganda. Some kindhearted people found a way to bring relief to the refugees, though, how could you ever truly find relief? Although you still have your breath, you feel as if your life is over. The shaking and the nightmares never end. Every time the wind rustles the bushes in your refugee camp, your heart pounds.

"Functioning As Normal Again"

Yet as the study shows in figure 10.1, the refugees did find relief. People self-score themselves, and this chart shows that they were miserably afflicted with PTSD at the beginning of learning the TM® technique

73

Decreased PTSD Symptoms in Congolese War Refugees
Through the Transcendental Meditation Technique

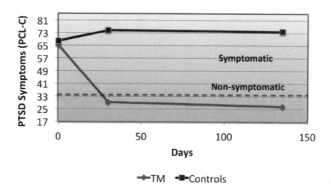

Reference: *Journal of Traumatic Stress* 26 (2013): 1–14.

Figure 10.1 For these PTSD Congolese refugees, symptoms were gone after 30 days.

and completely symptom-free after 30 days of practice. Their symptoms began to lessen within ten days! That is not a misprint for ten years or ten lifetimes. I warned you it seems incredible. But this is what happened.

What do these refugees say about the TM® technique? Esperanza states, as quoted on the David Lynch Foundation website: "The soldiers tortured me—almost killed me. Now, I feel like it happened to a different woman—not to me. I am a free woman."

In a video interview available on the David Lynch Foundation website, another African refugee, Pemba, said, "It was around 7:00 p.m. Soldiers came to our house. When they entered our house, they fired bullets. [She imitates the sound of the bullets: pah-pah-pah-pah!]. They took my husband, and I was left in the bedroom. There were six soldiers. I saw with my own eyes. One of the soldiers approached me and started to touch me. I pushed his hand away. When I refused, he took the gun and hit me [pah!] on the head. I fell down to the ground."

She doesn't remember what happened then. After that her mind was not working right. She had panic attacks. She couldn't stop thinking about her missing children.

These horrors occurred in 2008. Three years later she reported on what the TM® technique had done for her. "I can say that I am functioning normally again."*

What is startling, and certainly astonishing to a haggard and depressed person who has sought relief for several years, is hearing that the TM® technique works right away. It seems too hard to believe; how can this be possible? Yet, to stretch credulity even further, the technique works just as profoundly during the practice of a shiny new meditator as during the practice of an experience-softened, long-term meditator. (During the practice of meditation, the experience of the new meditator is as deep as that of the long-term meditator. During the day's events outside of meditation, there is a contrast in their experience. The long-term meditator maintains more calming and enlivening effects than the newbie.)

Instant Lessening of Anxiety

Neuroscientist Dr. Fred Travis tells the story of how surprised he was, after two months of studying brain scans of new and long-term meditators, to realize ("aha!") that the scans were identical. There was Alpha1 coherence throughout the brain. This means total brain functioning. It would be a remarkable thing to achieve such a state through meditation, and it is truly amazing. Earthshaking! And to achieve this immediately upon instruction of the technique, literally in seconds, is beyond earthshaking. It's just simply and utterly transformative and impossible for people to believe until their day of instruction when, in fact, they believe it . . . because they have experienced it.

Let's just suppose for the moment that, impossible as it seems, instant brain coherence does happen. Okay, but how? I wanted to know how it can happen that fast so that we can understand how this can occur for you and for me and for all of us. How could a few minutes

---

* https://www.davidlynchfoundation.org/africa.html

instruction in a particular meditation practice "turn our lives around 180 degrees" as one enthusiast put it. We want to know. Please, universe, tell us how could such turnaround possibly happen? How does it happen with respect to our persistent, burdensome, relentless worrying?

Okay, the research is there, but we need even more information to get at the question of why it works so fast. Even the study I'll introduce next doesn't show such stunning change, namely the instantaneous drop in anxiety many feel when they learn the TM® technique, but it shows a ridiculously big change in only a matter of days. An absurdly big change.

Science has verified that the TM® technique does lower anxiety. Laboratory research found, too, that the TM® technique especially lowers our worries with people with a *lot* of anxiety. Figure 10.2 is a chart of the study of the drop in anxiety when people practice TM, which appeared in the *Journal of Alternative and Complementary Medicine*.

Now, this study doesn't show how fast the effects can happen. But the Uganda refugee study demonstrated it. What this study does show is the remarkable thing we observe every time we instruct people in the TM® technique: People who are really a wreck have a remarkable recovery. It's as if they have emerged from a fog into a sunny day. Teaching the TM® technique to these people who seem to be basket cases can be like raising Lazarus from the dead, especially when you consider how long they have been plagued with extreme anxiety.

My wife and I taught TM® to school kids in Kingston, Jamaica. These kids practically had to climb razor wire to get out of their neighborhoods and into the school. Some of them were homeless, and often kids came to school hungry. Walking to school was running a gauntlet. They knew they better know the shortcuts and be able to run fast. If we whispered their TM® instruction to them, they'd turn from edgy and difficult into pussycat-style people. And it's the instant change part that's best.

"I'm just so nervous about this," a person said before I taught him. "You nervous now?" I asked at the end. "Nope." Now I ask this every time someone has reported that they feel tense before learning the technique, and they always, *always* tell me that they don't anymore.

Effects of TM on Trait Anxiety (Stress)

(PTSD, Prison Inmates, Anxiety Patients)

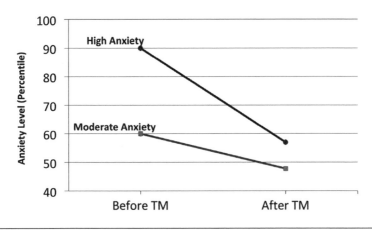

Figure 10.2 There is a dramatic drop in anxiety for those doing the TM® technique.[3]

Fortunately, Dr. David Orme-Johnson et al. did their meta-analysis of 16 anxiety studies shown in figure 10.2 and found that the TM® technique works, and it especially works on people who are seriously anxious.

Literally Decreasing the Stress Hormone

Let's get some more science in here. There's a pretty key piece of evidence, shown in figure 10.3 that something happens to these anxious folks. Scientists looked closely at how cortisol reacts to the practice of TM®. As I understand it, they had people spit into a test tube before doing the TM® technique and then again into a clean one afterward, and they measured how much cortisol was in each one. The study shown in the chart here compared their level of cortisol before TM® and their level during the remainder of the day.

There it is: a big decrease in cortisol for the TM® meditators compared to those who do not do the TM® technique. It's easy to glaze over the scientific research and forget the reality of what it means to have more or less amounts of cortisol in the body. We need to understand

Lower Cortisol Throughout the Day
Calmer Style of Physiological Functioning

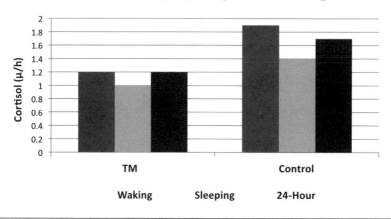

Figure 10.3 Calmer in the daytime, calmer in the nighttime, calmer all day long.[4]

that cortisol is nice in some conditions. It gets us focused. It gets us fired up. But it doesn't take too much for it to make us edgy, which is a colorful word for being anxious. Cortisol is there coursing all through your body, and how do you blot it up if you want to get rid of it? Good luck. I don't think even the antianxiety pills like Lexapro can wipe it up, but rather override it (they kind of bully it away).

But the body does somehow magically dispose of cortisol while we're doing the TM® technique. If the TM® technique did nothing else, it would be totally worth having for its cortisol-alleviating capacity alone. A stress blotter-upper. Awesome. And the change happened in the experiment called "Lower Cortisol Throughout the Day" within the 20 minutes it takes to meditate. (Presumably the drop in cortisol happens even faster than 20 minutes, like right away, but they apparently don't ask the people to spit the second time until they're done meditating.) The study also found that the drop in cortisol lasted for a while during the rest of the day.

Okay, just one more scientific study to look at before getting back to our pursuit of an explanation for how fast it works. Given how many people flock to mindfulness, this result is worth noting. As shown in figure 7.3, the TM® technique reduces anxiety more than mindfulness. When you consider that mindfulness has the same effect as sitting with the eyes closed, this study shows the advantage of doing the TM® technique versus closing your eyes and relaxing.

And what about the instant relief that the teacher of the TM® technique sees every time he or she or they conducts an instruction? The new meditator sees that the troubled, jittery, unmanageable brain comes to heel. Against all odds, and contrary to the experiences of a lifetime, a person smooths out and smiles and feels a deeply physical easiness and comfort. It's instant. It seems absurd. It seems impossible. And yet, it's real.

How could those victims of the Congo atrocities possibly recover at all, let alone recover quickly? They cannot recover by just forcing a change in mood by chanting, "I want to be happy. I want to be happy. I am happy. Yes, I am happy." The change has to be deeper than being in a different mood. The change has to be a fundamental change in the cells and tissues and hormones. The change cannot be anything we are accustomed to in ordinary life or we would all get this easily. It has to be extraordinary. Extra-ordinary.

CHAPTER 11

Diving Inside—the Possible Fix

"Words are just that—words! . . . signposts to get to a point and the experience is MUCH GREATER than the words! And yet I yearn to say that I feel love. I have these experiences of heavy heavenly vibrations all over my head, the amazing feeling of the tension being released from behind my eyes and nose air passages, being cloaked in this light of love, and I do not want to say words. I just want others to experience it for themselves. It is interesting to feel such passion about something soo natural, so innocent, soo loving. Maharishi is absolutely correct in (humorously) saying you cannot forget the experience of the self; once you dip into this ocean of nothingness you can never forget how refreshing the water is."

JEROME BUCHANAN, Professional Fighter

With those legions of distressed people that fill our introductory lectures, we're generally faced with a uniform, sometimes downright hostile look of distrust. People are just plain doubting that getting relief from this is possible. Who can blame them? These people are like the wounded ward in a war movie. They've been through a nightmare. They are skeptical beyond words, and while it is true they've managed to drag themselves to this meeting, they're basically done with the whole deal. "Whatchya got?" they're asking, with the implication that "It really can't be anything." But so many people have told them to try the TM® technique that they reluctantly come for a quick listen.

One person, an ex-Jehovah's Witness canvasser, told me that she didn't accept the invitation to remove her shoes because she wanted to be prepared to run out of the meeting at a moment's impulse. (She's still doing the TM® technique several years later.) What is it, then, that we're offering these inveterate worriers and panickers? Transcending is what we're offering. But "transcending" is only a word until they learn the practice and have the experience.

Just Thinking Doesn't Do It

"Look, I know how to meditate," the average Joe or Jo on the street will say. "First, you sit with your back straight. Second, you close your eyes. Third, you focus on your breath. Fourth, you try not to think about anything at all."

They've tried it or had someone teach them an approach something like this. Their conclusion was often "I can't do it. It doesn't work. It's a waste of time. I don't like it at all."

People wonder what this technique could be that has people dropping their anxieties rather quickly. The TM® technique can't be the old "sit with your back straight," which people sometimes refer to as "real meditation." Let's look at the reality of what it is.

"Transcending," Not "Just Thinking"

"Everything went black," a woman said, a few minutes into her first meditation. She was fully awake. She was enjoying herself. She had not fallen asleep. But she had slipped into a place that was different from ordinary thinking. And there, in that slipping inside, is the complete uniqueness of the TM® technique.

"What was that? Was I asleep?" people often ask me.

"I felt like I was floating." I hear this all the time.

The first difference or, if you want to say it, the only difference about the TM® technique and most other forms of meditation—what people refer to as "real meditation" when you sit with your back straight and focus on something rather than just thinking hard—is that with the Transcendental Meditation® technique you transcend. Generally, you don't think "maybe I transcended." You are more likely to think "What was that?" or "This really works." Or "This is different from what I expected."

Transcending is going beyond. It's not an intellectual thing. If it were, we could all just do it. We'd "think outside the box." Oops, nope, that's still intellectual. How do you even do it anyway? Fine, maybe you come up with a new idea about how to explain it. "Maybe you are breaking boundaries?" No, not if they are just fresh ways of thinking. Perhaps "open new gateways?" "Expanding the envelope?" Nope, nope, and nope. This rich, tantalizing, precious thing of transcending is not thinking in a new way.

Nor is it, as is often said about the practice, stopping your thinking in some way. It's a fresh thing. It's different. It's not what you have known already. It is experiential.

Fall Asleep in Body, and Become a Living Soul

Of course, there have been instances of transcending in human history. Lots of them. Gosh, probably everyone has had instances of it. (But try and snag this. It's like catching a fly with your bare hands. I know one guy who could actually do that. Just one, though.) William Wordsworth expressed the experience of transcending absolutely blow-by-blow perfectly in his poem "Lines Written a Few Miles Above Tintern Abbey." Here's what he said:

> . . . that blessed mood,
> In which the burthen of the mystery,
> In which the heavy and the weary weight
> Of all this unintelligible world,
> Is lightened:—that serene and blessed mood,
> In which the affections gently lead us on,—
> Until, the breath of this corporeal frame
> And even the motion of our human blood
> Almost suspended, we are laid asleep
> In body, and become a living soul:
> While with an eye made quiet by the power
> Of harmony, and the deep power of joy,
> We see into the life of things.

Talk about relief from worry. Here it is. Lightening the weary weight of this unintelligible world, oh, yeah. The world is so unintelligible that we cannot even get oriented to start fixing ourselves. Could you get relief anyway if you transcend? How we would love that. Bottle that, if you could, and you'd have the ultimate sedative. Induce that in a therapy session, and you're in demand across your city and the region beyond. The suspended breath he's talking about? It happens in the TM® technique. The lowered blood pressure? The lowered heart rate? All of these happen when practicing the TM® technique.

Maybe the experience is what was always called mysticism. "Mysticism" generally describes something abstract and vague and uncertain. The term means different things to different people and means nothing at all to many people. In the TM® technique, on the other hand, the abstract experience is describable, measurable, and repeatable. If it is mysticism, it is scientific mysticism. Medical mysticism. But don't call it mysticism at all. It is transcending. Scientists like to call it restful alertness. William Wordsworth experienced a profound state of restful alertness.

But here's the thing. Try on your own to fall asleep in your body and become a living soul. Maybe we trick ourselves and say, "Oh, I think I am doing it." We almost certainly are not doing it. Close your eyes and lower your breathing and your heart rate. Maybe you'll lower them a little, but not nearly what you do during the TM® technique. Figure 11.1 shows how breathing slows much more during the TM® technique than during simple rest (sitting with the eyes closed).

Another study, "Effectiveness in Reducing Trait Anxiety," that was shown earlier in figure 7.2, indicated that a practice that does not include transcending really amounts to just relaxing comfortably and closing the eyes. The "placebo" is just sitting with your eyes closed, and all the other approaches tested had no more effect than the placebo.

So transcending makes all the difference. And it happens to people in their very first session of actual instruction in the TM® technique. I mean, so many people have been living for decades, through lifetimes really, and have never had the experience of transcending or have only randomly experienced it once or twice. Even Wordsworth, who predated formal instruction in the TM® technique, couldn't transcend at will. Quite the opposite. He drew upon the memory of an instance of it, but that was mostly from his intellect and not from true transcending.

As teachers of the TM® technique, we hear many surprised and delighted responses to transcending from those who are just beginning:

- "Wow." (That's a common one.)

- "The room got bigger." (Great way to describe the expansion.)

Increased Physiological Relaxation
Meta-Analysis of 32 Studies

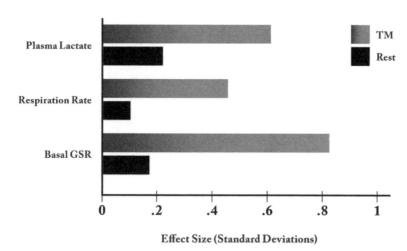

Effect Size (Standard Deviations)

Reference: *American Psychologist* 42 (1987): 879–81.

Figure 11.1 During the TM® technique, rest is twice as deep as with just eyes closed.

- "I felt like a medicine ball balancing on the head of a pin." Why not? There's the localized, familiar us, but it is widening its container (hence "medicine ball": heavy but expanded).

- "Everything slowed down, then I disappeared." (Love that one.)

There have been thousands of expressions like this—actually millions, as ordinary people take instruction in the formal Transcendental Meditation® program as taught by Maharishi Mahesh Yogi. They suddenly have their own experience of transcending and grapple to find words to capture the ineffable yet scintillating and, yes, worry-free time of being without the everyday world. Move over, Wordsworth. A new generation of man is having the Tintern Abbey experience, and that emerging crowd doesn't have to climb a few miles above a church to do it.

The Power of Brain Coherence

What else? What else other than transcending could possibly be different about the TM® technique? Well, you can't see them by yourself, but your brain waves are different from ordinary thinking when you do the Transcendental Meditation® technique. Brain waves tell the tale. They're like a little lie-detector test. Are you really transcending, or are you just fooling yourself and trying to fool everybody else? Get hooked up to an electroencephalograph and find out just what is going on in your brain.

In their seminal study, Dr. Fred Travis and Dr. Jonathan Shear compared the brain waves in the TM® technique, in concentration, and in guided meditation. You can see their results in figure 11.2.

In the Transcendental Meditation® technique the brain waves line up. (The TM® technique is the bottom one on the chart, "Automatic Self-Transcending"). That experience of floating, of being free, of being timeless, of operating in slow motion, shows up on this "lie detector test" of the EEG machine. Alpha1 waves are the ones where your worries go away and you slide into a blissful state. Seriously. It's blissful. The suspension comes in the alpha1 coherence. There it is, right on the computer monitor, in black and white. Really, It's just the transcending that tells the tale of how the Impossible Meditation works its wonders. "Transcending" is all the explanation we need for how the TM® technique is different and how it transforms lives.

In the Transcendental Meditation® technique you actually dive below the surface of life into an Alice-in-Wonderland world of ease and bliss and happiness and floating. It's quite a world in there. Astrophysicist Dr. John Hagelin, the head of the TM® program in the US, is fond of explaining how much more powerful creation becomes the deeper we go. The surface level, where Newton got bonked on the head with an apple, has enough laws and equations to drive a high school kid nuts, but Newton's world is just on the surface. Go to the molecular level, which

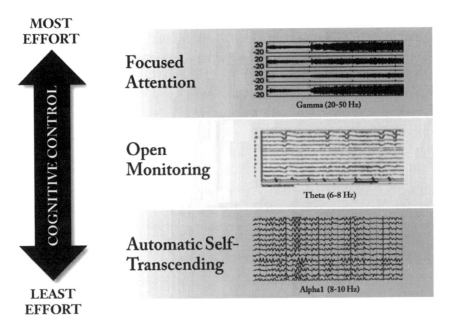

MOST
EFFORT

COGNITIVE CONTROL

Focused
Attention

Gamma (20-50 Hz)

Open
Monitoring

Theta (6-8 Hz)

Automatic Self-
Transcending

Alpha1 (8-10 Hz)

LEAST
EFFORT

Reference: *Consciousness and Cognition* 19, no. 4 (2010): 1110–1118.

Figure 11.2 Alpha1 coherence (bottom) during the TM® technique. During concentration, gamma waves, and during guided meditation, theta waves.

is like setting something on fire instead of just pushing it around, and you have a whole new level of power. Setting something on fire really gets the molecules doing their thing.

Go to the atomic level. It took our best scientists years and a lot of tests in the desert to split the atom. It's a tightly wound little devil. The atomic level is a million times more powerful than the molecular level. Go to it and wow, the world is different. Softer. Sweeter. Expanded. Truly nice. Wait, there are subatomic levels. Ya gotta love the names of those particles that live at that level —quarks and leptons and the famous Higgs boson. Oh, my goodness, those levels are powerful. Later in our time together in this book I just can't contain myself, and I tell you what bliss is like at those levels and what happens in a body swelling with love. Scientists build mile-wide machines just to play with those subatomic particles and try to separate them even further. Those subatomic particles are another few million times more powerful than the atomic level, if you can imagine that (and don't mind if you can't, because nobody can).

Then, astonishingly, there is a level that you can't even measure except by extension from the levels we can see—that is, a unified field level or (I love this name) a superstring level that is basically all-powerful, infinitely powerful, unimaginably powerful.

Use *that* level to combat your anxiety instead of using some handy, thinking-level platitude like "I am great." You know, if you could really dive into that unified field level, you'd give your anxiety really something to reckon with. Your persistent, nagging, ever-annoying anxiety might just disappear instantly the way people often say it does on their day of instruction.

Over all these centuries we have been trying to find relief from this untouchable human problem of worry, which is often incessant worry. Now we have the answer. Fill the body with bliss. Worry melts away. The anxiety forgets about itself and disappears. How do you fill the body with bliss? Well, just get the stress out of the way.

What is different about how this bliss-creating technique, this transcending, operates when obliterating stress, the bane of our existence? Stuff happens to us in life, as we remarked earlier. Trying to eliminate stress as we usually view stress is like fighting a swarm of mosquitoes with a laser beam. Life happens. The tax man cometh. We trip and fall. People let us down. Stress is out there waiting for us, and it pounces. Just as the TM® technique is special, doing what seems impossible by propelling us into the transcendent (whether we want to go there or not), the TM® technique is special in isolating stress and rubbing it out—step by implacable step. Everybody wants to get away from stress. The TM® technique, believe it or not, is a stress Roto Rooter.

CHAPTER 12

Dissolving Stress,
Not Just Dodging It

"I learned the TM® technique with Jim and Nina. My biggest problem
in life is being ADHD. I find myself all over the place throughout the
day, never finding a calm moment. That 20-minute meditation is the
greatest 20 minutes of the day for my head. It's my time to relax. I can
do it almost anywhere. I find that calm space and when it's over, I feel
more focused. I'm almost 60 years old. My biggest regret was not trying the TM® technique earlier in my life. I'm loving it."

DENNY TEDESCO, Producer, "The Wrecking Crew"

"I'm just under so much stress," people say, and they really don't see
any way out of it. A woman came to one of our meetings with hopes
that maybe (but probably not) the TM® technique could give her some
relief from the stress of her job. She is a lawyer and wanted me to picture her life. "You have to go up against people," she explains. "It's
confrontational a lot, and it can get nasty."

"We'd like a million five for damages."

"And I'd like to own the whole city of Los Angeles."

"We'll be filing the papers tomorrow if we can't get an
agreement today."

"We've already filed our papers to ruin him."

Conversations like that are her everyday life. I hear a lot about
people's problems at work. "I spend two hours in traffic just to get to
work, and another two hours to get home," people lament. If there's
an accident, it takes much longer.

"We typically work 14-hour days," report people from the film industry who are makeup artists, hairdressers, and grips, as well as the directors and producers. "Everybody wants a piece of me," a producer might say. "The actors, of course want this, but the camera people are after this, too, and the business folks are breathing down my neck."

Stress is caused by messy situations, and they are part of life, right? An online dictionary defines stress as "a state of mental or emotional strain or tension resulting from adverse or very demanding circumstances." Yeah, except what if those circumstances happen every day, all day, and you can't get them to go away so you can earn a living.

One day I happened to be in Seoul, S. Korea, or rather one night. It was about 2:00 o'clock in the morning, and some highly disturbed person was moaning and crying out for everyone to hear, "I've had all I can take. I've had it. I'm sick of this. Isn't there any help? There isn't. Oh, God. Oh, God." He was speaking in Korean, but this has to be roughly what he shouted for a long time. Know what was weird? Nobody reported him. Nobody came to drag him away. He was just this outcry in the night, and he was just saying what many who heard him were thinking: "Life is miserable. It's impossible. And the only way out is even worse than the problem."

Suffering from stress is our reality. You get it at work, for sure. Your boss demands too much. She is completely deaf to any explanations you might have. She's a quivering stress ball herself, so how is she supposed to be all smooth and easy for anyone else? No matter how hard you work, you come up short. The threat of getting terminated is an all-time guillotine you live with, and if it does happen things will get worse.

How about home with the family? If you've never been a parent, it's difficult to understand how much work children are. "Daddy, I need money for lunch." "Mommy, my shoes are worn out." "Daddy and Mommy, my teacher says I can't read." "I hate you." "Don't get near me." It's endless, and the truth is you also get pretty sick of complaints from your partner.

So you decide to take a vacation. You fight traffic to get to the beach. You get such a sunburn the first day that you just want relief.

You lose your wallet. The kids stay out too late, and you worry. When they come home, they look suspicious, as if drugs or even worse wrong behaviors have been in play. You long to be back at work.

Stress has you, coming and going.

Not Out There—in Here

Stress, everybody thinks, is all those unrelenting, painful situations that you can't fix. Transcending can't fix that. The traffic and the ungrateful kids and the imperious boss are on the outside. Transcending happens on the inside. However, the Transcendental Meditation® program, even in the face of stress, boldly offers a fresh perspective and a solution. "Stress," it says, "is physical." "Wait a minute. What are you talking about? Stress is my boss. Stress is my husband. Stress is the dent in my car. Stress is my out-of-range utility bill. *That's* stress."

"No," insists the TM® program, the all-time solution to human anxiety. "Stress is not stress unless it leaves some impression on you." "What?" If it's an overload, it's a stress, and if it isn't, it's not. Take, for instance, getting fired. Now mostly, yes, abrupt termination will put you into a funk. It will give you tightness all over your body and a serious frown as you go about your life. It will cause your prefrontal cortex to overreact, or perhaps to shut down altogether. Nobody likes getting fired.

Does stress make an impression on your nervous system? You can't change the circumstance. I mean, maybe you can, but in this example it's too late for that. You're fired. You can pretend that it doesn't bother you, but you'll fool exactly nobody with that. And words, we have established when speaking of self-help books, are no solution to stress. Stress in the form of outside circumstances is complicated and unrelenting. TM® ignores all that. It works from the inside.

According to the Transcendental Meditation® program, stress is physical. It's knots in our nervous system. When we get more pressure than we can handle, those knots form. "I'm burned out," people say, in a metaphor that nicely captures the idea that stress actually deposits itself in our nervous system. "I'm toast," we say. "Cooked." Well, that definition of stress doesn't change what is happening outside, but it opens whole new vistas of hope, genuine manageability, a light at the end of the tunnel for dealing with those outside disasters and mini-disasters and annoyances.

If you could somehow become smooth and easy inside, a flexible Mr. or Ms. happy-go-lucky-no-matter-what, take-things-as-they-go kind of person, even the firing might be just, as they say, all in a day's work. It might not be a source of worry at all. "How was your day, honey?" "Fine, except I just got fired again." If you are a stressed-out, taut piano wire inside, it's lights out when the firing is announced. Your misery may last weeks, months, a lifetime. "Pass the bottle. Pass ten of them. What am I going to do now? I am so ruined. Somebody please help me." And you go out on the street and cry and lament.

What if, miraculously, you somehow are no longer a piano wire inside but a lake? Make that an ocean. Throw a rock into a lake, and the disturbance subsides pretty fast. Throw it into the ocean, and the ocean doesn't even shrug. It doesn't notice. Your little rock is nothing. Life's various mishaps and disappointments, by the definition of the TM® program, are not extremely stressful events when we have become an ocean inside. Fine, but you don't become an ocean inside by pretending to be one. What do you do? Well, with a little transcending, things can change inside.

A Full Frontal Assault on Stress

We have pointed out that the TM® technique is not just some vague attitude but is measurably physical. Heart rate slows. Breath rate slows. Cortisol—miserable, anxiety-creating, frenzy-making, malicious cortisol—decreases. Youthfulness increases. Surely, in all that, there is heightened flexibility of the body. How about a study where we see the TM® technique affecting the DNA level? Such a study even exists.

News flash. You don't affect the level of gene expression with some fancy trick. You can't change it with a sledgehammer. You have to get the body operating on its finest level to change the DNA level because DNA is the lamp at the door between pure consciousness and the expression of the body. Now we have research showing that just such an intimate, fine-level change happens during the TM® technique. Note, especially, that the scientist W. Supaya working with Dr. John Fagan and others says that the TM® technique affects the response to stress. Restful alertness is another indicator of this blithe adaptability, this cavalier flaunting of the everyday stressors and going on unaffected in the midst of the chaos that is ordinary, everyday life.

One research study found that that there is increased blood flow to the frontal area of the brain during the TM® technique. That's inner awareness, and a good thing. It means being calm, not freaking out when threatened by some bully in line at theater. It means being on top of things—being the one keeping his or her head when all around him are losing theirs. The same study found that simultaneously there is decreased blood flow to the back of the brain (these parts of the brain make your body more active or less active). That is, during the TM® practice your body is calm while your mind is aware. That's good for handling stress. The meditation itself is an escape from stress, and some of that "lively chill" state carries over into your day, too. Your firing might not seem particularly overwhelming.*

Another study, by scientist Dr. David Orme-Johnson, "Autonomic Stability and Transcendental Meditation®" reported "autonomic stability" in meditators using the TM® program. Autonomic stability refers to all the things we don't think about and don't control—heart rate, pupils dilating, digestion churning away, even secreting or not secreting stress hormones. "Being chill" is a modern way to describe this stability, and research shows that we get that from the TM® technique. Don't you love the thought of packaging that California-style laid back quality into your life? You can be, historically, classically uptight, impossible to be around. Pipe in a little bliss from transcending, and happiness runs all through your nervous system. You may maintain your former exterior, a bit imposing, but the steadiness and imperturbability creep in. With each meditation you become less uptight, with a dramatic improvement with your very first meditation when the contrast with your former self is greatest.

---

* The study confirming this is by Mahone, M. C.; Travis, F.; Gevirtz, R.; Hubbard, D.; fMRI during Transcendental Meditation practice. *Brain and Cognition* 2018, (June), 123, 30–33.

Here is one chart from the study by Dr. Orme-Johnson, which, especially if you're at all in a technical mood, is quite neat. People often report to me that, thanks to the TM® technique, they are less reactive. And wouldn't you know? Scientists have measured it.

Figure 12.1, titled Conservation of Adaptive Reserves, shows the data that demonstrates autonomic stability. We are less reactive, which, in the experience of it, is really sweet. Who wants to be knocked off the rails by every mosquito's wing that lies on the track (a loose paraphrase of something I remember from Henry David Thoreau)? Okay,

Conservation of Adaptive Reserves

Autonomic Stability

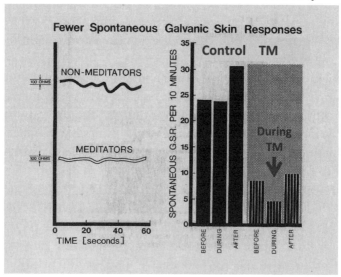

Mediators have fewer spontaneous stress responses than controls
outside of meditation, which decrease even further during TM practice.

Reference: Orme-Johnson, D.W. "Autonomic stability and Transcendental Meditation," *Psychosomatic Medicine* 35, no. 4 (1973): 341–349.

Figure 12.1 Autonomic stability, a k a being chill. Seriously less reactive.

God bless Google. Here is the original from *Walden*: "Let us spend one day as deliberately as Nature, and not be thrown off the track by every nutshell and mosquito's wing that falls on the rails."

"Galvanic skin responses," are caused by instances when you get upset, "flip out" and "Lose it." We hate 'em. And we cut them down as we grow in our inner reservoir of quietness. The scientists measured it. TMers are more chill.

I love another study that says doctors become less stressed and depressed when practicing the TM® technique.*

Doctors. I mean, they're cool in spite of themselves, but they aren't always cool in demeanor. It's hard to be a doctor and get all that adulation and be holding people's lives in your hand all day long and not have a little bit of excessive self-confidence creep in—A little bit of dismissiveness, which really isn't cool. But docs become cooler with the TM® technique.

The TM® technique is good for nurses in stress, too, and of course nurses do a lot of the real work in hospitals anyway, which is fine. And they stay nice. We meet lots of nice docs, too, of course. There is a new (2022) study looking at the effects of the TM® program on stress in doctors, nurses, and physician assistants working in the Covid-19 crisis. The researchers found a significant reduction in burnout, depression, anxiety, stress, and sleep disturbance.

The TM® Technique Stress Pump

One scientist has even used the term "stress pump" to describe what happens in the body during the TM® technique. Choosing her words carefully, another TM® expert suggests these terms to describe how the TM® technique dissolves stress. "As Dr. Fred Travis and other researchers have described, in the Transcendental Meditation® technique, the mind automatically transcends to finer levels of thought, and the body settles into a unique state of restful alertness characterized by a marked reduction of arousal and an increase of global integration of

---

* Loiselle M, et al. "Effect of Transcendental Meditation on Physician Burnout, Depression, and Insomnia: A Randomized Controlled Study." In preparation for publication, 2018.

brain functioning. In this state of restful alertness, the body's intrinsic self-repair feedback loops detect and repair imbalances, normalizing stress in the nervous system."

How awesome is that! If you could do it, actually dig down and Roto Rooter stress out of your body, thereby rendering yourself cool as a cucumber under pressure, wouldn't you do it? Systematized coolness. We're missing a great opportunity here. "Come and get your stress pump. Roto Rooter your nervous system." It would be a million-dollar marketing campaign. Even "self-repair feedback loops" sounds like a wonderful thing to have operating. The body is self-repairing anyway, but the deep rest of TM® strengthens such self-purification.

The body during TM®, ridding us of detritus in various forms that make us nervous, angry, anxious, actually reverses the effects of stress. The effects of transcending during the TM® technique are the opposite of the effects of stress on the body, as shown in figure 12.2.

Once we see stress as physical, the whole ballgame changes. You can't change your boss, or at least not easily and not without a lot of messy stuff. You can't trade in your children, who probably wouldn't mind, if they even noticed. You can't successfully train your husband not to have that second nightcap. You can't transcend the traffic on the 101. (It's been tried. Take the back roads. The city streets. Doesn't work much because Waze is sending everyone there.) The IRS is notably lacking a sense of humor. If you try to manage the challenges in your life on their own level, it's like pushing around the sand on the beach. There's just more sand. Sure, there's stress management, and you can cut back here and cut back there and avoid this and minimize that. But basically, it is Sisyphean. Hopeless.

When you are looking to manage yourself, on the other hand, instead of trying to get rid of stressful situations on the outside, you're playing a whole new style. Don't eliminate the stressors. Make the stressee (which is you) impervious. Use autonomic stability. Profound inner restfulness. An all-time chill.

The TM® technique does more than make you calm inside even under duress. It actually clears out that physical stress from the body. What does the body do when it gets rest? It takes care of itself. Give it *deep* rest, and it takes care of itself more. It purifies itself. The TM® tech-

The Psychological Effects of TM
Are the Opposite of Anxiety

Anxiety	TM
• Increased respiratory rate	• Decreased respiratory rate
• Increased heart rate	• Decreased heart rate
• Increased blood pressure	• Decreased blood pressure
• Increased muscle tension	• Decreased muscle tension
• Sweaty palms	• Dry palms

Reference: *American Psychologist* 42 (1987): 879–881.

Figure 12.2 Anxiety affects us one way, the TM® technique the opposite way.

nique, which according to certain indicators is rest that is twice as deep as the deepest sleep, remakes not the outer stresses but the inner ones.

When stress is on the outside, it's just out there. Fighting all that outside disruption is like Bill Murray fighting the gopher in *Caddy Shack*. You're outmaneuvered. Might as well just give up. When it is on the inside, you can clean it out step-by-step, automatically, by giving the body the deep rest it needs as the basis for its housecleaning. Stresses dissolve. As for you—it's all about calm. Easy. More and more stress-free.

Seeing stress as physical knots in the body, snarls that you can pump out, completely levels the playing field for fighting stress. Once stress is inside, we have a chance. In fact, we're in control, and we can systematically lower the stress day by day until it's gone (if you can even imagine such a thing). With the impossible technique, we don't even have to know where it is hiding, what pernicious organ is secretly causing us all that angst. Still, in its comprehensive improvement of the body, the TM® in effect does hunt down that organ, that unfixable fear center. And fix it.

CHAPTER 13

Taming the Wild Amygdala

The Many Health Benefits of the
Transcendental Meditation® Technique

"Since the 60s and 70s, I have been aware of the Maharishi and Transcendental Meditation®. More recently, I came to wonder what I had been missing. Learning TM® from Jim at my local center was one of the greatest things I've ever done. A real 'a-ha!' moment. Negativity, worry, and stress dissolve with the daily practice. Life gets better. Jim said it would be like this!"

RALPH DAVIS, Software Consultant

There are lots of things we'd like to fix in the body. You'd think that fixing any of them would help to make us less anxious in life. It doesn't take much to set us off about our health. Health concerns are a complete anxiety stimulator. Health imbalances can throw us into a tizzy.

"What's that feeling in my chest? Am I having a heart attack?" "I think I feel a lump in my lymph node. Where is the lymph node anyway?" "I've got a twinge in my knee. I'm going down. I know it. I'll be using a walker, then a wheelchair. This time next year I'll be completely immobilized."

"What's 'chronic fatigue syndrome?' I'm feeling pretty tired. It's lasted for a couple days. I should see a doctor." "I had my hernia fixed, but they say that mesh isn't good anymore. I'm feeling some sensation down there. I probably should go to the ER." "My eye is cloudy. Yeah, might be going blind. Then what will I do?"

Studies have shown that daily doses of the TM® technique strengthen our health at the core. What does it do for our anxiety to be rock-solid healthy? If you know you're healthy, you still might worry about your health. But you know deep-down that feeling well keeps us from going overboard with the worrying.

When you're doing the TM® technique as an antidote to your worry, you're also taking care of a lot of the health concerns you would otherwise be worried about. For those distressed petitioners from the opening chapter, the talk mostly goes right over their heads when I tell them about the health benefits of practicing TM in our introductory talk. ("Maybe I'll get into the health stuff later," they often seem to be thinking. "Right now, I'm floating on an ice floe and it's melting. Just get me off.") Still, I want to tell them that the abundance of health research in our time holds so much promise for keeping them on an even keel and enjoying themselves once they start the TM® program.

Healthy Brain Waves

One thing that happens during the transcending experience of the TM® technique is brain wave coherence. As you are becoming peaceful inside, the brain activity in literally all the parts of the brain also settles down. Instruments that measure electrical waves in the brain show that during transcending the brain waves line up. An incoherent brain becomes coherent. That brain coherence that arises in the TM® technique doesn't just soothe your worry. It strengthens the overall performance of your body. Figure 13.1 shows the correlation of brain coherence and benefits to your mind and body.

There, on the right, are the correlations with less worry. Coherent brain waves correlate with "Decreased Neuroticism." Other studies show that they correlate with decreased state anxiety and decreased trait anxiety, terms the scientists use to refer to what most of us call "stress." If you want less worry in a more direct form, there's "increased emotional stability." We could all certainly use that. But intelligence goes up. Creativity increases. "Neurological efficiency" goes up. Neurological efficiency sounds like the opposite of being sick.

The TM® technique, increasing coherence as it does, helps us across the board. Maybe, in that broad sweep of our systems, it fixes the root culprit of our worry. But what is that root culprit? Perhaps the immune system is the culprit in our body. The immune system consists of the bone marrow, thymus, lymph nodes and vessels, spleen, mucous membranes, tonsils, and skin.

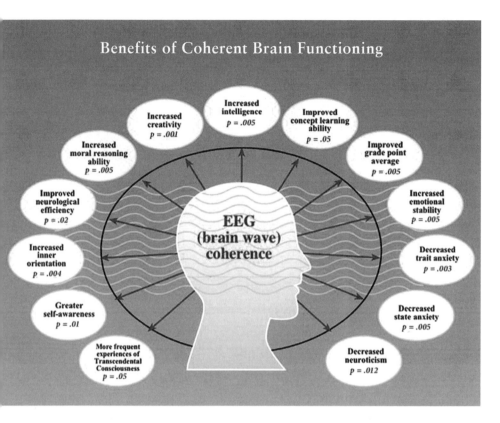

Figure 13.1 Brain-wave coherence is good for all kinds of things—but especially, for our current discussion of "anxiety" (lower right). This chart has evolved from the efforts of several scientists collaborating and making adjustments over time.[5]

Strengthening the Immune System

Given that the immune system fights everything and could be considered our body's own internal security system, fixing it would seem do a lot to take care of anxiety. And your immune system gets stronger with the TM® technique. So, while you're using a natural technique to soothe your anxiety, you're building up your resistance to disease.

Figure 13.2 gives information about a study of the immune system conducted by a team of eight doctors in Spain who found that the TM®

A Stronger Immune System
Through the Transcendental Meditation Technique

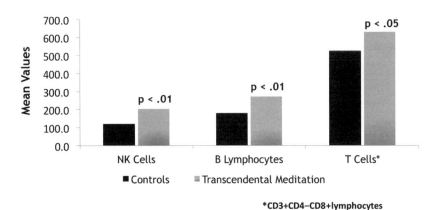

TM increases white blood cells that defend the body from infection and cancer.

Figure 13.2 The TM® technique strengthens our immune system.[6]

technique practitioners have more of three different types of white blood cells that defend the body against infectious disease, cancer, and foreign invaders.

The specific details are that those doing the TM® technique had more of the following:

T cells (CD3 + CD4 − CD8 + lymphocytes) that destroy virally infected cells and tumor cells;

B lymphocytes, which identify and neutralize foreign objects, such as bacteria and viruses;

Natural killer cells, which provide rapid response to virally infected cells and tumor formation.

A study of the immune system conducted by a team of eight doctors in Spain found that the TM® technique practitioners have more of three different types of white blood cells that defend the body against infectious disease, cancer, and foreign invaders. You can read specific details about how this study showed an increase in the ability of our cells to fight disease when practicing TM® in the endnote about figure 13.2 in the back matter.

Lowering Blood Pressure

Are you concerned that blood vessels have become too restrictive? When we worry, the numbers sure spike. Get at the root of elevation of our blood pressure, and maybe we're getting at the root of our anxiety. As Figure 13.3 demonstrates, the TM® technique does a good job at reducing high blood pressure, for sure.

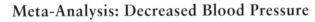

Meta-Analysis: Decreased Blood Pressure
Transcendental Meditation compared to other techniques

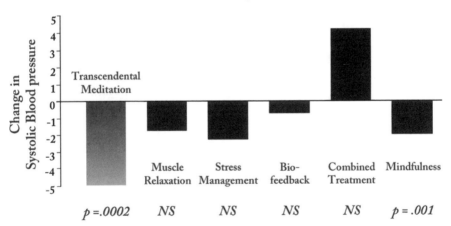

107 studies identified, 17 RCTs analyzed, N=960

Reference: Rainforth, M.V., et al. *Current Hypertension Reports* 9 (2007): 520–528.

Figure 13.3 Practicing the TM® technique lowers blood pressure.

Lowering Cholesterol Levels

The TM® technique lowers cholesterol, too. I've had meditators tell me that their doctors, quite surprised at their lower numbers of cholesterol, had to change their prescriptions. I want to pause just a little bit because lowered cholesterol from meditating is not intuitively obvious at all. We take statins for this purpose since they block an enzyme in the liver that makes cholesterol. According to César Molina, M.D., F.A.C.C., as quoted on the TM.org website, "The Transcendental Meditation® program has been associated with a drop in total cholesterol in research studies, but there has never been a large, formal study comparing it against statins." While it may not be known how the TM technique does this, it does lower cholesterol. Maybe it decreases cholesterol in some better way than the statins. Dr. Molina says as much, suggesting that transcending "may be more powerful than statin drugs in improving outcome," but then concedes, "we don't have that data."

Lowering cholesterol levels naturally is pretty cool and is one more reason that the TM® technique lowers the risk of heart attack (and we do have data about lessening the risk). If we improve the numbers for our cholesterol, we surely worry less, but cholesterol is this slippery substance that does not seem to be the ringleader in causing our worry about our heart. It is just an attendant player, maybe even just a symptom.

What about hardening arteries, related to levels of cholesterol in the body, being the cause of anxiety? Consider that actually opening up the arteries does happen when practicing the TM® technique.

Figure 13.4 presents a study of the effects of the TM® Technique on the carotid artery. In the words of the doctors who conducted the study, "a health program that included the Transcendental Meditation® technique, a heart-healthy Ayurvedic diet, exercise, and herbal food supplements significantly reduced the thickness of the 'intima media,' part of the lining of the carotid arteries, an effect known to correlate with reduced risk of heart disease and stroke."

Opening up arteries is a big deal, as in . . . really hard to do. Maybe scraping them out would be good but would be messy and risky. I guess stents are a mechanical way to open arteries, but the stents don't really change the constitution of the artery. Exercise is said to do it, though too

Reduced Risk of Atherosclerosis
Through the Transcendental Meditation Technique

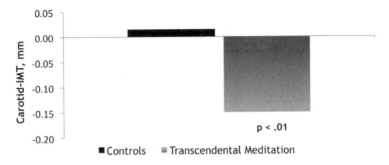

TM, along with a heart-healthy Ayurvedic diet, exercise, and herbal food supplements significantly decreases blockage to the carotid artery (carotid-IMT), a correlate of artherosclerosis.

Figure 13.4 The TM® technique opens up the arteries.[7]

much running doesn't seem worth the trouble and might not open the arteries that much. Change our diet? Maybe. But who has the patience, and we always cheat on our diets. Related conditions, like the health of our heart muscle itself, do get better with the TM® technique.

Furthermore, a 2019 study in the journal *Ethnicity and Disease* showed that the TM® technique prevents hypertrophy of the left ventricle in the heart, which is quite significant because hardening of the ventricle is a precursor to heart attack. All these generalized effects from the TM® are great to know about and certainly contribute to our overall health and even to our autonomic stability. A healthy person is a less worried person, and a healthy heart definitely helps keep us smooth.

Helping the Heart

It's fun to think about holding death at arm's length by doing something like softening the left ventricle. But among all the research on the effects of practicing TM® is an especially noteworthy study that showed decreased heart attacks and death from heart disease for those who practice the TM® technique. See the data in figure 13.5.

Reduced Rates of Death, Heart Attack, and Stroke

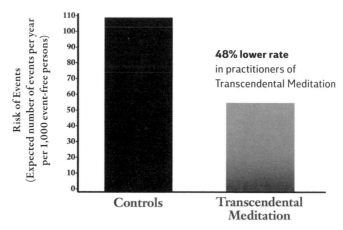

Reference: *Circulation*. Cardiovascular Quality and
Outcomes 5, no. 6 (2012): 750–58.

Figure 13.5 The TM® technique lowers the risk of heart attacks, strokes, and death.

The health results just go on and on. Name your health concern, and you can find that the TM® technique makes it better. Here is evidence of our across-the-board improved health. Reduced hospital admissions for those who practice the TM® technique are shown in Figure 13.6.

What does lower hospital admissions mean? Hospital admission is a pretty solid statistic. It's not just the result of some questionnaire where someone talks about how good he or she feels. We are asked about the condition of the following parts of our body: "Intestinal," "Nose, throat, lung" (that familiar ENT doc we all know, with the lungs thrown in), "Heart" (and now we're getting somewhere, because we tend to sit up and take notice when our hearts are under performing), "Genital & Urinary" (a little embarrassing, and we don't tend to go there, but we don't want something going wrong there either, and things go wrong less with the TM® program), "Body Injuries" (and I love that one, because, well, why do injuries happen? Chance, sure.

Decreased Hospital Admissions Rate in All Categories of Disease

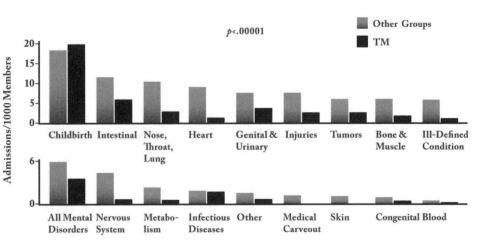

Reference: *Psychosomatic Medicine* 49 (1987): 493–507.

Figure 13.6 People who practice the TM® technique make fewer trips to the hospital than those who do not practice the TM® technique.

Bad karma. But also from a fogged-over brain or overstressed mental functioning, even panic—that is, the kinds of things that transcending corrects, and the list goes on). It's a study based on hard data. People have to be pretty bad off before they go to the hospital at all, people who practice the TM® program are bad off less often than those who never immerse their brains in the transcendent.

There are hundreds of studies of the health benefits of this practice. Organizers of the TM® program have compiled eight hefty journals of research so that a world in search of reassurance can go straight to the source to see, in the language of the scientific age, the actual, nitty-gritty research that has been done.

Yes, such comprehensive studies assure us that something in us is regulating our stress. But what? Knowing we are at less risk for heart attacks if we practice TM® certainly makes us less anxious as the days go by. But lowering the risk of a heart attack is not helping us to isolate the physical organ causing our distress, which I will now discuss.

The Culprit of Anxiety Is Tiny and Hidden.

Here's a physiological explanation of what might have happened so fast to help the recovery of those refugees in Uganda. There's a fear center in our brain, the amygdala, the area in our brain involved with processing our emotions and detecting threats. Its job is to scare us into action. "Hey, idiot, there's a bus bearing down on you. Jump for God's sake." The fear jolts us, and we jump. Apparently, for the sophisticated analysts (the neurologists and such), there is more to anxiety than just the reactions of our fear center. But the amygdala is a big player. So, basically, when we're worried, the amygdala gets our body pumping out norepinephrine, acetylcholine, dopamine, serotonin, and cortisol. Can't you just feel it? Even trying to pronounce those substances can get you trembling. Have them swimming around in your system, and you're ready for a serious alcoholic drink, or several.

You pump out adrenalin, the hormone secreted by our adrenal glands. You need it when you're in a wrestling match and you're in a choke hold and you gotta do something to keep you from dying. You can use a little of it in all kinds of circumstances. Everybody knows about adrenalin, which is probably why the scientists don't talk about it anymore but instead call it "epinephrine" since not everyone knows what that is.

Whatever you call it, you get good and jazzed when your fear center kicks in. Pumped. Maybe even out of control. You might engage in "Fight or flight," neither of which is particularly fun, but one or both might be necessary when danger strikes (or when there is absolutely no danger, but you've managed to get yourself thinking there is). You might even panic, an extreme form of anxiety.

Well, what if you could, say, massage the pesky, hyperactive little organ in charge of making you feel frightened? Put a little ointment on it to calm it down? Talk to it? Sing the little amygdala a lullaby? Good luck, because it's like an unruly teenager and won't listen to a thing you say. It will do the opposite of what you want just to spite you. The amygdala is an ornery, stubborn, demanding little organ with a distorted sense of its own worth. Unfortunately, it has the clout to back up what it says.

Would self-help books be useful? This is not likely. Tell your amygdala that most of the things you worry about never happen anyway. It doesn't care. "Well, this one might," it persists, stubbornly, wantonly, cruelly. Your analyst can't do much of a job on resetting the amygdala either if all he or she does is talk about your problems. A little selective serotonin reuptake inhibitor (a tranquilizer) might help because it's a chemical (and so is the adrenaline) but the SSRI just increases one chemical, serotonin, while leaving other sometimes troublesome ones to wreak their havoc.

What do you do? Some neuroscientists theorize that the TM® technique actually resets the amygdala. That sounds pretty abstract when it's just words, but maybe it's not so abstract for those frenzied worriers who transcend for the first time on their day of instruction in the TM® technique. There is a saying from the Bhagavad Gita that "Even a little of this dharma delivers from great fear." What is dharma here? It's the TM® technique and, more specifically, the transcending during the TM® technique. Let's even say it that way: "Even a little of this transcending delivers from great fear." It's in the ancient texts. The problem of applying this aphorism from the ancient texts until now has been that the words alone don't do much for you. The problem has been that the experience of transcending itself had become lost. But now it's back.

If these words describing transcending were just some fleeting intellectual exercise, then, no, this wouldn't do much at all to the amygdala—maybe make it flinch for a beat or two before getting back to pumping out stressors as much as it wants. But think about those coherent brain waves during the TM® technique, brain waves that happen instantly when a person begins a session. Transcending with the TM® technique is a dive into a river of such soothing peacefulness that your amygdala quiets down like a trusting baby hearing a lullaby.

And here, then, is the explanation of how the change could happen so fast when people learn the TM® technique. Although I would hate to lose you, you could just leave right now and find a center that offers the TM® program right near you and begin to transcend. The transcending, actually allowing the mind to move to an inner field of coherence and bliss, is that single experience that is monumentally powerful. You can't overstate it. When we transcend, what do we connect with? We connect with the infinitely expanded reservoir of endless energy and intelligence that structures every last atom of the ever-expanding universe.

When those stressed people, our friends from the introductory living-room lecture, come in for their first day of an actual experience of transcending, all their amygdalae take a bath such as one that this organ of fear has never taken before. Their amygdalae stop pumping out fear and just go silent like a disturbed pussy cat petted and cooed at by its owner. There's instant change. A transformation from misery to bliss, a 180° change on the spot. Not that the people know that the culprit in the brain has quieted down, but they sure know they have calmed down. Now you can meet some of them.

CHAPTER 14

Finding a Way Out: Real Solutions

A YELP REVIEW

"I was in a very dark place before I met Nina and Jim. I had really bad anxiety and depression. I had no appetite and couldn't sleep. I tried prescriptions, didn't work . . . tried different types of meditations, didn't work . . . therapy, didn't work . . . I thought nothing was going to heal me until I met Nina. After my first initiation I had this bliss come over me, I hadn't felt happiness in a very long time. I had my appetite back and my sleep back, after the very first initiation! TM® changed my life!!! I went through a deep purification after a couple days and Nina was there for me and guided me step by step. I honestly don't know where I would be right now if it wasn't for Nina and TM®! Nina and Jim, these people are here to genuinely help you, nothing else. And after your 4-day class, they provide lifetime support for free for the rest of your life! No therapists or doctors provide that. I wish everyone could come to Nina and Jim to learn TM."

All right. Let's take stock a bit. All those folks I introduced you to in the first chapter were anxious. Grieving. Couldn't sleep. No sense of self. Depressed. Unemployed. Feeling dark, dark, dark. Could barely think. Contemplating suicide. Completely freaking out.

And here I stood before them, dressed in a suit and tie, smiling, cracking jokes, citing scientific research, and promising them relief. Heck, to be honest, I had to hold myself back from pleading with them to learn the technique. They had no idea where they were standing. They were on the brink of eternity, just a few syllables away from a bliss like they had never imagined.

What happens to them and others like them when they learn? Relief would be enough in itself. But *instant* relief, without a pill? Come on. We've mentioned it before in the case of the Congolese refugees. But they are an extreme case. What happens for ordinary, stressed-out soccer moms or an everyday wealthy, successful, hardworking grandmother in her sixties. She's good at her business, where she works with her husband marketing a good product. She gets along with her grown daughter and loves to buy toys for her grandkids. She drives a handsome car. And, oh, yeah, she's completely miserable. How much worse can it get than having panic attacks when you completely lose control, feel struck with terror from head to toe, and collapse in sheer helplessness a couple times a day? "I thought I was having a heart attack," a fellow told me of his first panic attack. You think you're dying. I mean, going through that is pretty bad, right?

The hardworking grandmother came in to learn the Transcendental Meditation® program because nothing had worked to stabilize her and make her feel better, and the panic attacks and anxiety kept driving her to try things. Friends told her to try the TM® technique. Of course, she didn't expect it to work. But she would pretty much try anything even halfway reasonable.

Here's the remarkable part, and why I hold out hope for those sad people I introduced you to. She came in for instruction in the TM® technique, bringing fruit and flowers that is our custom on their first day. She received her instruction and then—listen to this—she astonished herself by saying the amazing words: "It's gone. The anxiety is gone. I feel great. I'm happy." This woman is a real person, and a real person who was plagued by anxiety for fifty years and saw it disappear in five minutes. I met with her for four days altogether, and during that time she remained completely anxiety-free (and, believe her and me, before this she had never gone four days straight without feeling some intense anxiety).

From 8 Grams a Day to None

I have another story of success that I like a lot. It's about a woman who had worked herself silly in life, including working herself into a frenzy of anxiety. Tina was a medical doctor, which usually means, of course, a proud and adulated leader of the pack. In fact, she had left her previous practice, no doubt in frustration over lack of freedom to do things right and was in the exasperating and exhausting process of setting up her own office. She measured her anxiety the way doctors do, in the number of grams she was taking of Xanax, your everyday benzodiazepine (in more familiar terms, a "sedative"). She was taking 8 grams a day, and, as she explains for the lay audience, "That's a lot."

How much was she taking when I saw her three months after her first meeting with me? I had to reread my notes on this myself to be sure I remembered correctly. The amount was none. She went from taking 8 grams of Xanax to taking none. Don't do this at home without consulting your prescribing physician and, obviously, without starting up the little engine of the TM® technique that removes anxiety.

Who else makes it into the catalog? I've taught this to a couple of thousand people, teaching along with my wife, and every one is a story of the decrease of anxiety. As I've mentioned, I've made it a habit of addressing their anxiety before they begin their instruction, and I ask them after their day of instruction whether they feel smoother, happier, and less anxious. You can see them take a quick inner glance before saying "Yes."

Julian's success is another great story. He's okay in business. Why not? He's employed and paying the bills. He's a self-described addict who had been sober for 23 years when he came to the TM® technique. (Addicts are like Marines. Once you are an addict, it's for life even though you may not act out anymore.) He wasn't aiming to strengthen his anti-addiction tools, although the TM® technique would have helped him with that. What he wanted, oh so desperately, was relief from his anxiety. On instruction day, right away, the anxiety disappeared. When I saw him six months later, he said that the fear and anxiety had come back by about 20 percent, but hey, that's pretty good and, truth be told, he may not have been doing the TM® technique as regularly as he had at first.

Gerson was a man who came to the TM® technique looking for a specific weapon to deal with a defined problem. He was 49, handsome, proficient, and generally good at everything, as is the case with Type A personalities. But he had not been a star at his practicum for getting his aviator's license. During his flying test his anxiety caught up with him. His brain started fogging over when he made his first mistake at the controls. Things went from bad to worse, and in short order he heard from the examiner, "Hand me the controls," code, of course, for "you flunked."

He arrived at his meeting with the fruit and flowers that candidates bring to their instruction on the first day. He proceeded to receive the weapon to serve his specific purpose—the practice of TM® technique to relieve his anxiety so he wouldn't lose his cool in the air again. The tester had told him to come back in six months, which was the standard time for a non-meditating exam flunker to recover from the stress of it all and regroup before tentatively trying again. For Gerson, the time back to another test was about two weeks, which was as soon as they could do his test again after his instruction in the TM® technique. Did he pass? Can monkeys climb trees? He sailed through the exam, buddying around with the tester both before and afterward and, thanks to the TM® technique's seeming miraculous antianxiety properties, emerged from his practicum a licensed pilot.

Gerson had experienced generalized anxiety since ninth grade. He had been reluctant to put into play the advantages his good looks and business success might give him in his social life. It didn't help that he also had sweaty palms. But once he learned the TM® technique his palms were dry.

"Twenty minutes with Jim, and I was fixed," he quipped a month or two later. (It's not *me;* it's the technique.) I haven't heard yet whether his luck with making new friends and meeting women has changed. He didn't even need luck. He just needed the courage. But I am sure if he stayed regular in the TM® technique, his success would include enjoyable relationships.

Relief from Sleeplessness and a Fluttering Heart

My compilation of relief-from-anxiety stories goes on and on; there's a story for each of the thousands I have taught and for each of the millions worldwide who have learned the TM® technique. I don't like to go too long without telling the story of Carolyn, a Hong Konger living amidst the swirling throngs of people who make up what is probably my favorite city.

Carolyn was suffering, and she was caught in a multiplying series of difficulties. First, of course, was her anxiety. She said she had an ogre for a boss, a completely demanding and insensitive man who gave her obstacles to make her feel pressured at work. She had every reason to be anxious about her job.

Her situation was made worse because she was also afflicted with atrial fibrillation. Do you have any idea how scary that is—even terrifying? As your most indispensable organ goes into its irregular fluttering, you are reminded over and over of human frailty and your own danger of having a sudden loss of consciousness. Isn't that enough? But another problem was that she was unable to take refuge in that one nurturing, protective, escapist practice we all love when we can get it: sleep. She couldn't sleep well. In other words, she had insomnia.

But Carolyn was one of the most persistent, downright not-to-be-denied-no-matter-what candidates I have ever met. She took an immediate liking to my wife, Nina. She wanted to learn from Nina, and she wanted to learn from her right away. She made her commitment and left only to purchase the requisite fruit and flowers once the appointment time was set in stone. And learn she did.

I think I'm still trying to shed the weight I gained from her gratitude. Every time she came for follow-up, which she did for weeks until my wife and I left Hong Kong, she brought the most sumptuous, creamy, light-as-a-feather pastries. A dozen of them. She just needed to let the universe know how utterly and exhaustively she had managed to shed her stressors. It was chicken-and-egg as to which came first—relief from anxiety, or relief from the a-fib, or the increasing slumber she enjoyed at night. It doesn't matter which came first or whether they all got better simultaneously and then reinforced one another in her recovery from anxiety. *They all got better!* She got her life back because she began to practice the TM® technique. It even would have helped her tolerate her boss, and manage him, but that is another story and fodder for another book.

Okay, just a couple more stories, or maybe a few because there are so many good stories of the people I worked with who received anxiety relief. There's Sharon. She's from Lebanon but is American now. She was starting to be pretty familiar with the ER docs in Woodland Hills, where her family would take her when they could find no other way to rescue poor Sharon from her panic attacks—make that "frequent panic attacks."

I have her on record saying, "I haven't had a panic attack since I learned the TM® technique," and she said that months and then a year or two after learning it. Wow! Are you kidding me? And she came in one day to tell me about her car accident. She rear-ended someone, which is an everyday occurrence in LA. No shame in it at all. Traffic is always stopping in the most unexpected places. Glance down to adjust your mobile phone and look up to see yourself butting someone

However, here is her story. Such an untimely event in the past, pre-the TM® technique, would have put her back in Woodland Hills at the ER. For starters, it would have put her back home where she would curl up in the fetal position and wish someone could figure out how to rescue her. Not this time. She got out of the car, comforted the woman driving the other car—which in the past would have been a huge expenditure of psychic energy—and then, wonder of wonders, went on to do the Christmas shopping she had set out to do with her dented fender flapping in the breeze showing everyone what had happened (but as I said, in LA that's just the lay of the land. No one bothers to look).

I like the story of Allen, too. He seems like the picture of confidence. He has that millennial air of seeming to be proficient, quite on top of things, and not needing anyone to show him the way. It's a wonder he even started the TM® technique. But he did, and that self-assurance I am speaking about turned out to be only skin deep. "I've been depressed for years," this Hollywood film editor put it. "But I've been happy ever since I learned the TM® technique."

Susan was another nice person but was a sad case who practically had to be brought to her instruction in the TM® technique in a wheelbarrow. She was just marinating in her own misery. She quickly reversed everything when she learned the TM® technique and is the one who, on the day after her first session, was dancing around the kitchen and singing for joy.

Okay, I'll stop. I want only to include the woman who visited me before she moved away because she wanted to tell me, "You gave me my life back." She also mentioned she had dismissed her therapist. The logic was simple. She went to therapist for her anxiety. The TM® technique fixed the anxiety. There was no more need for the therapist.

Relief from Anger, Sleeplessness, and Alcoholism

I also want to mention the U.S. Marine who said after learning to practice the TM® technique, "To be able to have relief from agitation, and have relief from anger, frustration, sleeplessness, alcoholism, and drug addiction—that's huge." What a story he had. Most of the folks in his group—the Wounded Warrior Battalion at Camp Pendleton in California—were understandably nursing their wounds. Anxiety was only one of their problems and not the major one, either. PTSD was rife. So they often didn't want to do much. This man, unlike the others, was developing and marketing an app. He took up bicycling. He went square dancing. When he was last heard from, he was heading off to Oregon to start an organic farm.

Thus the beat went on with instance after instance of relief from anxiety (and relief from depression and pain and (oh, wait, I want to tell you another one). How about the sex addict, miserable and by her own description "drowning," who is the one who said, "My life turned around 180° in one day."

But I was going to stop. This seems so improbable. Surely, you might think, I must be lying. All these people must be lying. But it's all true. They had been seeking relief from time immemorial or, more accurately, for as long as they could remember. They were usually skeptical. They just went through the motions of taking instruction. Then it all changed. The lights came on.

Why would they make this up, though? Nobody was bribing them. They have no apparent agenda. They're just everyday people who used to be miserable in their anxiety and, thanks to a single reason, are not anymore. And it happened almost instantly.

Do you recall the fellow who was 22 and was so anxious he couldn't drive? He came back to the center about a year after his meeting to learn TM®. He came by himself. He'd been driving for so long that he thought nothing of it. I had to ask him if he had arrived in his car because he forgot that there was a time when he was so frazzled and overcome with anxiety that he couldn't drive.

And the truth about Sam. Sam's a clown. He had the rare opportunity in life to attend clown school on a full scholarship. But that was a long time ago. When he winched himself finally into a meeting on the TM® technique, he wasn't a clown at all. He was working in banking. How did that sit with his entertainer self? He started the TM® technique, and he showed up for a meeting after a year or so, smiling, confident, and fresh from his Uber ride. "I have a part in SpongeBob SquarePants," he exuded, explaining that he had been going to auditions for 20 years before that and not getting parts. "The directors could smell the fear," he said. Well, the fear was gone after he began the TM® program, and his acting career was back. (That bump in the career is another effect I see all the time from those who learn the TM® technique, fodder for another book, too.)

Herald is a producer who hadn't slept in nine years. Is that even possible? Herald is the successful producer whose film is high on the all-time list of movies about the music industry. He had severe insomnia. Most of us have had that experience, usually for one night, or part of the night. It's worse than nightmares. It's a waking nightmare. Aren't we told you go crazy if you don't sleep for many days? It makes people psychotic. We need the sleep to release the stress of life. After Herald learned the TM® technique he began sleeping, not every night but at least sometimes.

Steve is the one who couldn't stand to sit by the window on a plane. His situation, he would gladly tell you, was hopeless. You can't talk yourself out of it. It was a phobia. He could try sitting in the unwanted seat as a test case, and inevitably it would be embarrassing as he would begin to sweat and become a medical emergency. And what happened after learning the TM® technique? He came in smiling to a meeting and said he had sat in a window seat on the plane with no problem.

Happiness Instead of Depression and Grief

Grief. What about grief? Now, there's a disabling condition. The loss is so irreversible, the pain so overwhelming. One woman whose husband had died after a long illness came in to learn TM®. He was a musician with all that often goes with it—personality, spontaneity, joie de vivre. After he passed, which you cannot prepare for as much as you think you can, she fell into a depression and stayed there. For months. When she learned the TM® technique, just like that, the blackness lifted. She began to be a happy person again. She prepared a sendoff for him featuring his musician friends, and she had plenty of energy for the task. Practicing TM® fixed her grief.

Instant relief. Anxiety, the age-old problem of mankind, making even the rich and powerful miserable amidst their grandeur, goes away. Sometimes the worry dissolves in the first instance of transcending with the Transcendental Meditation® technique. Such dramatic effects are hard to believe before you actually try the TM® technique. It's not hard at all to believe it afterward. Recently I asked a fellow who had been meditating for about two months about what benefits he was receiving. He paused and scratched his head a little. The silence became a bit awkward, putting pressure on him to speak. This was a man who was living at home with his parents and running a business with no customers and no income. His anxiety had been an everyday trouble for him. "Well," he conceded as if the changes were not much of a benefit, "The anxiety I was feeling is gone."

The Transcendental Meditation® technique as taught by Maharishi Mahesh Yogi quickly—often immediately—relieves us of even the most overwhelming anxiety and stress. And there you have it. You find yourself on Earth at one of those most rare and precious times when, with the small investment of a little preliminary training and then 20 minutes twice a day of a regular practice, you can be easy, happy, normal . . . the way you think most other people must be.

A Complete Makeover, not a Palliative

For the teacher of the TM® technique, the parade goes on day after day, week after week, year after year. Seekers arrive. The fashions change, sometimes with the locale. In SoCal it seems the women all have painted toenails and dyed and carefully styled hair. In Tanzania the woolen blanket is a popular mode of dress. If you set up in Colorado, people come through in climbing gear. In San Diego you might get a surfer coming to the talk with plaid shorts and a striped T shirt (and an amazing tan). In Manhattan you may get some buttoned-down types. In Hong Kong the same.

Obviously, ethnicities vary, and often you can't tell and would like to know where someone is from but think it might seem rude to ask. Perhaps someone is Polish, French, German, Ethiopian, South African, Kentuckian, South Carolinian, or Georgian (either type, from the country or the state). Or maybe someone is from Persia, Russia, Armenia, or California. The parade of people is endless in their coming and endless in receding into a past experience.

But the reason people arrive to see us is constant: the stress, the anxiety. And one amazing result is the same: the relief they receive, perhaps in the amount of a 25 percent, 50 percent, or 100 percent improvement of how they were before. Variations can occur from 25–50 percent and back to 40 percent, but nonetheless there is considerable relief from stress and anxiety. And another report is that this is constant. Nothing else has worked nearly so well. And here they all come, the seekers, often appearing desperate and often feeling desperate but hiding it well. And their teacher whispers a few gentle words to them, and they dive inside, and their life transforms.

"It changed my life," says Ellen DeGeneres, the great and famous Ellen DeGeneres. Here it is. What everyone is looking for. What everyone has always been looking for. Sometimes those with severe anxiety and panic attacks are fortunate because they are so motivated to find help that they are willing to try this too-good-to-believe technique. And, over and over, as they search for the right words to express their gratitude, they say to the person who has taught them the TM® technique, "Thank you. Thank you so much. I can't thank you enough."

When stress is gone, where does anxiety fit in? It doesn't. It just doesn't. What makes the stress pump do its work? Transcending. But what is fascinating is when the Transcendental Meditation® technique chills out the body, it doesn't just numb us. Oh, no, not at all. Quite the opposite, in fact. You heat up while you chill out. You don't really think Wall Street loves the TM® program for enabling a certain blankness inside, do you?

The TM® program is so much more of a makeover than a simple palliative for anxiety. It's a bottom-up changeover. I wish people were coming to the TM® technique to become great instead of just to fix their worries. But I don't know if I really wish this. I guess at some point most of us figure if we're not great yet—we're no Einstein or Shakespeare or Jimmy Kimmel—then we can't expect that. Besides, we're not feeling any urgency about our not being on a marquee or whatever. We'd like it, probably, but maybe not. It's the immediacy of the jitters and the insatiably buzzing mind that brings people in to the lecture. We have been focusing on a crowd favorite, anxiety, but depression closes in on many of us as well. Let's check it out before seeing how this immersion-into-the-deep inside helps to bring on success in our lives.

CHAPTER 15

Ending Invincible Depression

"To me, the most striking aspect . . . Is how fast the TM® technique began to work [on his depression]. With Jim the change was almost instantaneous, while Sara was feeling better within two weeks."

DR. NORMAN ROSENTHAL, author of *Transcendence*

In my experience, anxiety, for sure, is the main reason that people come in to learn the TM® technique. But depression is also a great problem for many and has its legions who have abandoned all hope. Can the TM® technique help depression, too? Depression often accompanies anxiety but can be less apparent than anxiety to the persons suffering from both afflictions.

Last Stop Before Jumping

"In September my grandfather passed away, and there were a few things about that which set me into a severe depression which no one noticed, not even my wife," reports writer Brian Baker on the TM® Blog, concluding, "The next week I took my first lesson. That was one week ago. I feel more awake, and for the first time in a very long time, I feel alive." If those words are not enough to influence you, here's more from Mr. Baker, "I can only speak of my experience, but the TM® technique was my last stop before jumping. I've backed away from the cliff in the last week and I'm now more comfortable in my skin than I've been since before my parents were divorced when I was eight."

The Harvard Medical School reports the following:

It's often said that depression results from a chemical imbalance, but that figure of speech doesn't capture how complex the disease is. Research suggests that depression doesn't spring from simply having too much or too little of certain brain chemicals. Rather, there are many possible causes of depression, including faulty mood regulation by the brain, genetic vulnerability, stressful life events, medications, and medical problems. It's believed that several of these forces interact to bring on depression.*

Yet the TM® program has reported amazing results, and I have seen them myself in people who come in to learn. The patient or a doctor doesn't need to sort it out. "Is it a mood disorder?" "Is it her father passing away, then her husband, and her cancer?" "Caused by side effect of the meds?" Transcend, and the field of pure consciousness sorts it out, even in cases that seem insurmountable.

The Great, the One and Only . . . Howard Stern

Howard Stern, revered talk show jock, reported, "My mother was very depressed because her sister died." She was so profoundly depressed, he relates in a YouTube video with Jerry Seinfeld, that his father came home and said to his wife, "Let's become alcoholics." The radio star said, "She tried psychiatry but was very closed off to it. Nothing worked."

You know how this story is going to end. One day his mother called Howard, sounding completely happy—organically happy. "I've started meditating," she said. What Stern told Seinfeld about Maharishi and the TM® technique is "She owes her life to him."

Here's another report from one of my favorite meditators. Well, actually, they are all my favorites. He told me, "I've always been depressed. I have depressive personality disorder." I responded, "Do you feel more upbeat now that you do the TM® technique?" He laughed and answered, "I'll never admit to that. You might jinx it." After a nearly lifelong depression the man was happy.

Yes, there is scientific research affirming the effect of the TM® technique against this unruly, unbeatable, ever-shifting condition. Some examples are shown in figures 15.1 and 15.2.

---

* Harvard Health Publishing, Harvard Medical School, Blog Article "What Causes Depression?" June 24, 2019. https//www.health.harvard.edu/mind-and-mood/what-causes-depression

Decreased Depression in Government Personnel
Through the Transcendental Meditation Technique

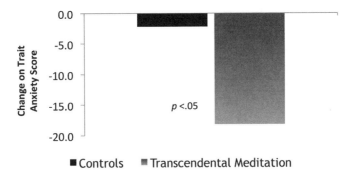

Employees of a high-security government agency reported to be highly stress-ful displayed decreased depression after practicing the Transcendental Medi-tation Program for three months, in comparison to control employees who participated in an educational stress-management program.

Reference: Sheppard, W.D., Staggers, F., Johns, L. "The Effects of a Stress Management Program in a High Security Government Agency," *Anxiety, Stress, and Coping* 10, no.4 (1997): 341–50.

Figure 15.1 **Employees of a stressful government agency showed decreased depression after practicing TM for three months.**

Short-term. Long-term. Intermediate-term. The TM® program is effective against depression, unlikely as that might seem. As indicated in figure 15.2, "Reduced Symptoms of PTSD in War Veterans," studies have shown the mental practice of meditation also helps other disabling conditions found in PTSD, including insomnia, alcohol addiction, stress reactivity, and our familiar problem of anxiety more than mind-fulness does.

As Robert Redford and Paul Newman say to one another in *Butch Cassidy and the Sundance Kid* when they cannot shake their pursuers, "Who are these guys?" What, we are asking, is this meditation thing? Are you kidding me about this?

Reduced Symptoms of PTSD in War Veterans

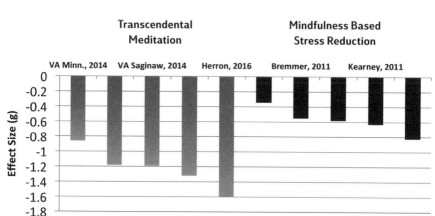

References for Studies: Brooks, 196: 626. Rees, 2014. *Journal of Traumatic Stress* 27, no. 1: 112–15. Rees, 2013. *Journal of Traumatic Stress* 26: 295–98. Kearney, 2013. *Journal of Clinical Psychology* 69, no. 1: 14–27. Bremner, 2011. *American Psychosomatic Society Conference*, San Antonio, Texas. Kearney, 2012. *Journal of Clinical Psychology* 68, no. 1: 212–15. King, 2013. *Depression and Anxiety* 30, no. 7: 638–45. VA Studies: *Meditation for PTSD demonstration project: Final report to Mental Health Services, Department of Veteran Affairs*. Rochester, New York: Department of Psychiatry at the University of Rochester; 201485. *Journal of Counseling and Development* 64: 212–15. Rosenthal, 2011. *Military Medicine* 176.

Figure 15.2 Decreased symptoms of PTSD, anxiety, and other stress-related issues in war veterans who practice meditation.

A Little Blood Flow Fixes It

What is going on in your body when someone is depressed? Neurologist Dr. Fred Travis explains it in an email to this author: "Depression is associated with decreased activity in left frontal areas. Those brain areas integrate and direct the functioning of other brain modules. Then emotional output, like depression, takes over the cortex and you cannot move. When you are tired or under stress, left frontal activation is also lower. So, often depression emerges when the person is tired or stressed. The TM® technique results in increased brain blood flow. It also keeps situations from becoming stress."

There, then, is the simple mechanics of how the TM® technique combats the mental health condition that Sir Winston Churchill called his "black dog." It's black, it's fierce, and it's unrelenting. But you can soothe it by increasing blood flow to the frontal areas of the brain. You can't will yourself into sending more blood flow to somewhere. But you can transcend, and this increases the blood flow where you need it. Amazing.

How does the TM® technique fare in comparison to therapy? Dr. James Krag reported this on the website TM.org, "Research also shows a decrease in depression with the practice of the TM® technique. For instance, in a study published in the *Journal of Counseling and Development,* patients suffering from post-traumatic stress problems who learned the Transcendental Meditation® technique showed significant reduction in depression after four months, in contrast to others who were randomly assigned to receive psychotherapy and did not show significant reduction in depression."

So, yeah, the TM® program works against depression just as it does against anxiety. Maybe you're not even sure which one you have or if you have both. You can target treatment for one or the other and miss the mark. Transcend, and you soak whichever one or ones you have in a field of powerful, transforming bliss. Yes, the TM® technique helps depression, too. Of course it does. If it just fixed bad things, seemingly impossible-to-fix things, that would be enough. But changing those things is only the beginning. It powers us up. Rewards keep cascading in. It can bring wealth and happiness.

Believe it or not, people can become great or, well, greater than when they started. Performance goes up. There is no theoretical limit to how high we can fly as we eliminate stress and get our brains working better and better. The popularity of the TM® program on Wall Street illustrates beautifully how the TM® program ups performance, stamina, and income and so much more than just our coolness under duress, and increased performance further helps that coolness.

PART IV

New Worlds Open Up

CHAPTER 16

Money, Money, Mo' Money

"Billionaire Ray Dalio, the founder of hedge fund behemoth Bridge-water Associates, has been practicing Transcendental Meditation® for 42 years. "Meditation, more than any other factor, has been the reason for what success I've had."

RAY DALIO, quoted in Julia La Roche article in *Insider*

The TM® program does more than melt away anxieties. It would be simplistic to say that it makes us rich. I know advanced TMers who are well-off financially and others who, in terms of their bank accounts, are just scrimping along. Lots of people think that tons of money, oodles and oodles of it, would take care of all their anxiety. We have established in chapter two that that is not true. Even the rich have worries. I met a guy at an intro lecture whose big problem was that he was ridiculously rich and therefore bored. Money might or might not help with anxiety. In either case, the TM® program helps with making money or at least with performing well in a job.

Being wealthy is good, but having a sharp competitive edge is good, too. Wall Street loves the TM® program for more than just enabling the peace of "inner silence," according to Richard Feloni, a writer for the Insider website (formerly called Business Insider). On November 2016 he wrote a piece for them titled "Transcendental Meditation, which Bridgewater's Ray Dalio calls 'the single biggest influence' on his life, is taking over Wall Street." Feloni's story was like a Who's Who of Wall Street with its compendium of heavy hitters who take the time from their horrendously overloaded schedules to practice the TM® technique twice a day for 20 minutes.

Deal with Challenges Like a Ninja

Ray Dalio is Founder, Co-Chairman, and Co-Chief Investment Officer of Bridgewater Associates, one of the largest investment firms in the world. According to bloomberg.com, as of February 2022 Dalio had given his Dalio Foundation almost 1.3 billion dollars, and he remains a strong proponent of Transcendental Meditation®. What kind of life do you have when your world is like this? Where do you begin to spend your money? But the interesting point is this. These guys like Dalio aren't just taking a tranquilizer in doing the TM® technique. No way. I don't know if they take tranquilizers or not. But they tell you that their purpose in practicing the TM® technique is to sharpen their edge—not to dull it—and it might rescue them from some slough of despondence that high-powered traders can slip into.

One reason Dalio likes the TM® technique, he told Feloni, is because it helps you deal with challenges like a Ninja. The deep, lively inner silence creates what he calls "a calm, clear-headed state so that when challenges come at you, you can deal with them like a ninja—in a calm, thoughtful way."

Mark Axelowitz is another trader Feloni talks about. I'm scared off immediately from looking at this guy because he's so imposing. Axelowitz works 18-hour days. Count 'em. But here's even more. He splits his time between Wall Street and Hollywood. They're not even on the same coast. Just the plane rides would do in most of us. Here are some of the shows he's been in—*The Comedian* (2016), *Burn Your Maps* (2016) and *Operation Cowboy*. (Okay, fine, I don't know them. But I don't watch enough TV.) What is a guy like that looking for from his TM® program? Probably not just a little quieting of the brain. How about endurance that he knows contributes to good health? How about, well, being "present" on the set and not only remembering his lines but adding something special to his role? Whether consciously or not, he probably appreciates the energy and focus the TM® technique brings him, not just the stillness and softness (which he also receives, of course).

Be Like Bolt, Bezos, and Gates

Here's another bit of research on the TM® program I want to mention. TM® helps us stay calm while in the midst of activity, and activity on a trading floor can be activity wrought to its uttermost. See figure 16.1.

As I've seen in many TM® meditators, practicing TM® increases energy. In the research shown, the energy comes from being calm and not wasting effort in fretting and doing useless things. We have to wrap our minds around such a thing. This "sedative" gives us more energy. It also increases performance. It doesn't just "relax" the brain. It gets the parts of the brain working together, such as being more focused and more creative and having more energy and being more calm *all at the same time*. Brain integration, now there's something. What kinds of brain functions do we get when playing them together all at once when we integrate the parts of the brain—like the violins and the cellos

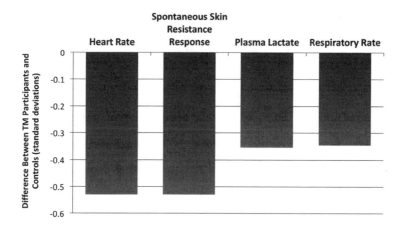

Calmer Style of Physiological Functioning:
Less Stress in Daily Activity
Meta-Analysis of 32 Studies

Figure 16.1 The TM® technique, the great chill-out practice, helps us stay calm in the midst of activity that is normally thought of as stressful.[8]

and the tympani and the flutes and the oboe and the tuba all working together in a symphony?

Another look at brain integration from the TM® technique is shown in figure 16.2. The technical terms, "frontal coherence, alpha relative power, and brain preparatory response," mean essentially what Dalio was talking about when he said people could behave like a ninja. The people whose results show up on this chart are focused; they're creative in a lively way, and their timing is great—they don't pounce until the right moment. Then, ominously and memorably, they do.

Holy smokes. World class athletes beat the ordinary athletes in brain integration. This makes sense. Top-level managers beat, you

Brain Integration Scale

*Frontal Coherence, Alpha Relative Power,
and Brain Preparatory Response*

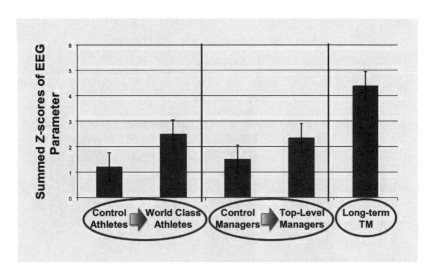

Reference: Based on the work of Fred Travis and Harold Harung and expressed in their book *World-Class Brain.*

Figure 16.2 Long-term TM® practitioners have more brain integration than other high performers (world class athletes and top-level managers).[9]

know, everyday managers. You would hope they would, though it often seems like some pretty incompetent ones rise quite high. Here's the stunner. Long-term TMers have more brain integration for success than the best in those other categories. That means a long-term TMer has more brain integration than people like Hassan Bolt or LeBron James (not necessarily them specifically) and also more than people like Mark Zuckerberg, or Jeff Bezos, or Bill Gates. Really? This is quite something. Once again it seems "impossible."

If you get the kind of brain integration and energy shown in these charts, you can be a force on Wall Street and perhaps quite a few other places. Being a force on Wall Street, you'll make more money. And having money, for all the tongue-lashing it has to take, does make life easier.

Here are a couple more of those Wall Street wonders who despite their incredibly pressured lives take time to close their eyes and transcend. Andrew Ross Sorkin, a financial columnist for the *New York Times*, explicitly makes the connection between the TM® technique and performance. Sorkin said, as quoted by Richard Feloni, "Trading is a mental game, and anything that gives you even a slight edge is valuable."

Didier Phitoussi has been in the hedge-fund industry for more than 28 years. In his interview with Feloni, he highlights the advantage of the TM® technique. Feloni reported Phitoussi thinks "TM® allows people in these situations to better deal with this stress and have a clearer head."

The TM® technique brings more than simple business success on Wall Street, though, not that such success wouldn't be a testament in itself to the value of transcending. I know many people who practice the TM® technique who've enjoyed the benefit of strong intuition, perseverance, creativity, and (another unsung benefit of transcending) just plain good luck.

When we worry, we often worry about failure. We frequently worry about money. "I'll never get that contract." "My boss hates me." "I'll never raise the money for this project." "Why was I left off that listing?" "Wait a second. Did I just do something illegal?" "We're going to have to lay people off. How's that going to feel?" "Why aren't they calling me back?" "If I don't raise this money, I'll be out on the street panhandling. I'll make a hand-lettered sign saying 'Anything helps.'"

Now, it's nice that the TM® technique calms the brain, resets the amygdala, lowers blood pressure, slows the breathing, and decreases the stress hormone, cortisol. Those changes bring immediate relief from anxiety. We know that success also brings relief. In a much less heralded stress-fighting benefit, the TM® technique helps us succeed in business without really trying. It makes us smarter, more competitive, sharper. It gives us an edge. It brings us, in many instances, money.

Being on top in business is obviously not the only solution to anxiety. As part of an overhaul to make you smooth in the face of the harrowing challenges of life, money is helpful. So is having the respect of others. The TM® technique, heightening our performance and thereby our self-respect and finances, is good.

If I had the clout, I'd lay to rest once and for all the misconception that the TM® technique makes us "stop thinking" or that it slows us down. No way, José. The TM® technique is this living paradox because it eases us inside while increasing our efficiency, our output, and our performance. Spread that high performance over a company, and that has to be good.

CHAPTER 17

More Money for Companies, Too

"The mechanics of the TM® technique foster sharper focus and broad awareness. Spontaneously (without thinking about it), we grow towards sharper focus."

Business consultant and former business professor
ANDREW BARGERSTOCK

Cut employees' stress, and a company thrives. Such is the current thinking. It's not as if business has not adopted the TM® technique. Oprah taught the TM® technique to her staff, as did Katy Perry. General Motors had a program. So did its competitor Toyota. Sumitomo in Japan also had a program. The TM® technique hit Wall Street big a few years ago with the multi-billion company Bridgewater Associates, founded by Ray Dalio, leading the way.

And *Variety* magazine in April 2016 broke the exclusive news that, as they put it, "Marvel's Top Executives are Obsessed with Transcendental Meditation®." I taught one of them myself. For its part, Marvel kept its TM® participation secret, and in general the TM® technique in business is largely a well-kept secret.

People Work Harder.

Here are ten ways the TM® program brings fixes to entire companies.

1. *Performance gets way better.*

Hard work is an often-overlooked benefit of establishing the TM® technique in business. The TM® technique heightens output. Workers are "clear." They're fresh. They're working at a job they like. Robert Daniels started out as a chimney sweep and in a matter of a few years built a successful company selling chimney supplies called Copperfield Chimney. "The secret to our success was hard work," he says. "The secret to the hard work? TM® twice a day every day."

Meditate so that you can work hard? Absolutely. Stress wears you down. It shuts down the brain. Under stress you just want to take long breaks, anything for some relief. The more you're free from stress, the more you get into your work. Resistance evaporates. You don't experience the work as work, but you perform beautifully. If you add the TM® technique into the daily routine of the workforce, the people just flat-out work harder.

2. *Workers think more clearly.*

As for fogginess in the workplace, we've all seen it. "I pulled an all-nighter last night rewriting the marketing material," a manager will report, looking every bit as bleary-eyed as such a daily routine would merit. How efficient is he or she in conducting that morning's meeting? How reliable are his or her decisions?

Or people cluster around the water cooler as if being at the workplace automatically means being at work. Their heads are just cloudy. The TM® technique lifts the fog. "I feel like I'm looking at life through a new lens," comments TMer David, a banker. "I went to take my usual afternoon nap," reports another new meditator, "but I just wasn't sleepy." For the TMers, clarity takes over.

What's lifting the fog worth in business? Without clarity, we see a lot of simple-minded decisions. I witnessed an instance at a TSA-point at the airport. Someone had mistakenly picked up someone else's C-Pap (a device to aid breathing). The stressed-out workers and manager did nothing to recover the lost device. They just mouthed platitudes like "It will show up soon." "Go to the lost and found." The device remained lost, and everyone was the worse for it. When you have lots of people putting in time, unthinkingly mouthing platitudes, not much really good happens.

3. *Creativity, so needed in the Amazon business world, goes up.*

Creativity seems to be turning the world around in business. You don't take taxis anymore. You grab a ride with your enterprising neighbor who drives for Uber. You don't go to a department store. You simply buy what you want online, and it appears the same day at your front door from Amazon. Maybe you don't stay at a hotel. Instead get a place through Airbnb . . . and save money.

Creativity is not just about having fun and being entertaining. It is literally about survival in a dog-eat-dog world. Who can begin to estimate the value of creativity in business? TM® practitioner Theodore, a real estate investor, often buys properties that others find worthless . . . and turns them into income producers. How? By being creative. Where others say, "I'd never buy that land by the Little League field. There's too much traffic in the summers," he says, "I can buy that land for a bargain. Nobody else wants it. I can make a few improvements and resell it, perhaps to a developer."

Meditating film producer David Lynch has immortalized one image for the value of the TM® technique and creativity in his popular book *Catching the Big Fish*. He says, "Ideas are like fish. If you want to catch little fish, you can stay in the shallow water. But if you want to catch the big fish, you've got to go deeper." Lynch is talking, of course, about the way that the TM® technique takes us deep into the mind.

Maharishi, during one of his press conferences early in this century, spoke about "Group Dynamics in the Corporate Culture." It is not the hours of hard work that matter in business, he said. It's the intensity of creativity put to hard work. Add the two together and you have a company that has a high chance of succeeding.

4. *Managers get clearer, nicer, and more effective.*

Not just the employees work better. Management rises to new heights. "The world-class executive search firm Korn Ferry conducted a study of close to 500 executives. They found that CEOs who were self-aware had 25 percent higher financial performance than those who weren't," said proponent of TM® and successful executive David Bishop, former head of Sony Pictures Home Entertainment and MGM Worldwide Home Entertainment, now an executive leadership coach heading up his own company, The David Bishop Group.

Korn Ferry Institute Study Shows Link Between
Self-Awareness and Company Financial Performance*

The Korn Ferry Institute analyzed a total of 6,977 self-assessments from professionals at 486 publicly traded companies to identify the "blind spots" in individuals' leadership characteristics. A blind spot is defined as a skill that the professional counted among his or her strengths, when coworkers cited that same skill as one of the professional's weaknesses.

The frequency of such blind spots was then gauged against the ROR of those companies' stock. The analysis demonstrated that, on average:

- Poorly performing companies' professionals had 20 percent more blind spots than those working at financially strong companies.

- Poor-performing companies' professionals were 79 percent more likely to have low overall self-awareness than those at firms with robust ROR. . . .

A study we reported in figure 16.2 shows increased brain integration in students who practice the TM® technique, and the effect is the same in managers. An integrated brain has perspective. It has self-awareness. It has compassion. Managers with brain integration are nicer, and they get better performance from their workers.

5. *Dumb Luck, that precious intangible, goes up.*
Way up sometimes.

Having your auspicious events in your life increase is just good luck, right? Sure, you hear the realists who say, "I make my own luck," and more power to them. But a promising opportunity is usually bigger than something we can make on our own. We can manage hard work ourselves. Those amazing strokes of propitious events that suddenly enable us to purchase a new home or find new friends or exciting business opportunities are, as the saying goes, made in heaven. They're beyond our individual efforts.

---

* https://www.kornferry.com/about-us/press/Los Angeles, June 15, 2015

Nothing can substitute for having good fortune, and coherence throughout the company heightens the possibility of things going your way. Meditating businessman Fred Gratzon enjoyed sudden success with his Great Midwestern Ice Cream Company when *People Magazine*, to his great surprise, branded his blueberry ice cream the best in the country. The TM® landscape has countless examples of what it refers to as "support of nature."

Business consultant Andrew Bargerstock speaks of the "total organizing power of natural law," that unseen organizing force of the coherence within a meditating company. Not only do events you planned turn out well, but unplanned good things happen, too.

6. *Companies stop wasting money on stress-related sickness.*

I don't think that health cost savings is a primary motivator for businesses, though maybe it should be. But the good old stress Roto Rooter of the TM® technique just makes people healthier. Many people I instructed in the TM® technique have told me, "I don't get colds anymore, and I used to get sniffles every time I turned around." And they sleep. They have energy.

First of all, then, the TM® technique relieves stress, and anxiety is the bugaboo of business these days. "U.S. workers are among the most stressed in the world, according to Gallup's latest State of the Global workplace report," states the CNBC.com website in June of 2021 in an article by Jennifer Liu. Her story also reports from the Gallup poll that "Some 57% of United States and Canadian workers reported feeling stress on a daily basis, up by eight percentage points from the year prior."

Stress causes sickness, ranging from colds and flu to cancer, diabetes, and heart attacks. Figure 17.1 gives data about the relationship between stress and illness.

The creator of this chart is Robert Herron, PhD. In his dissertation and published research, he has concluded that "The TM® technique reduces hospitalization, doctor visits, medical expenditures, heart attacks, strokes and deaths by 10 percent to 14 percent per year." The TM® technique in any company brings such improved health. Consequently, the TM® technique pays for itself in saved costs for healthcare,

How Stress Weakens Health and Raises Medical Costs

*Unemployment, home foreclosures, debts, declining economy
and standard of living, worry, wars, crime,
toxic pollution and food, and other major problems*

— Chronic Stress —

**Unhealthy Lifestyles
and Behaviors**

**Direct Damage to
Physiology**

Chronic Diseases

High and Rising Medical Expenses

75% to 80% of all medical expenses are due to chronic conditions

Figure 17.1 How stress makes us sick (and raises medical costs).

hospitalization, and our next reason for adopting the TM® technique—reduced absenteeism.

7. *People are happier and stop missing work so much.*

If people aren't sick, they come to work. According to Larry Comp, President of LTC Performance Strategies in Valencia, CA, the TM® technique reduces absenteeism and thereby saves money.

The U.S. Centers for Disease Control and Prevention, in fact, put the cost of absenteeism in the U.S. at $225.8 billion annually or, in terms of individuals, $1,685 per employee. Reduced absenteeism, then, is a second payback for the TM® program.

8. *And they stop quitting their jobs in frustration.*

Healthy employees remain on the job. Research like a 1995 study in the "Journal of Business and Psychology" reports that the TM® technique increases job satisfaction, a second way that the TM® technique keeps people on the job. Figure 17.2 shows a chart of increased job satisfaction, from the TM® technique's Center for Leadership Performance. I remember one fellow who came to learn the TM® technique and complained that he hated his boss. After his four days of instruction, he liked that same boss (and she had not changed in any way).

What does it mean when employees stay on the job? You don't have to pay for advertising to find someone new. You don't lose the productivity of the one who was up to speed. You don't have to spend weeks or months training the new employee (who also might get dissatisfied and quit).

Gallup News brings to light the astonishing costs of replacing employees. In a March 2019 article titled "This Fixable Problem Costs U.S. Businesses $1 Trillion," it was estimated that "the cost of replacing an individual employee can range from one-half to two times the employee's annual salary." If that annual salary is $50,000 (which it probably won't be any more in this inflating economy), and if the

Increased Satisfaction with Professional and Personal Life
Through the Transcendental Meditation Technique

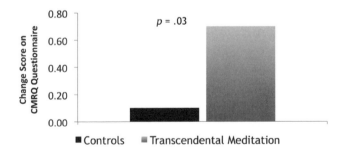

In addition, this study of executives and workers in the automotive industry found that after three months of regular practice of the Transcendental Meditation technique, participants showed increased professional and personal satisfaction, in comparison to controls from the same work sites.

Reference: *Anxiety, Stress and Coping: An International Journal* 6 (1993): 245–262.

Figure 17.2 The TM® technique makes people happier with their jobs.

company has ten employees, the company could have "turnover and replacement costs of approximately $660,000 to $2.6 million per year." Turnover is costly. Avoiding it saves money, and the TM® program can help to keep employees at their jobs.

9. *The workplace becomes a nicer place to be.*

"Group coherence is a powerful tool for organizational effectiveness," attests Bargerstock. He tells of a FedEx driver who, after a few months of visiting a company every day where the people did the TM® technique, asked simply, "There is something different and very positive about this office. What is it?" Coherence is tangible, says the professor. Nurses, that heavily challenged class of nurturers and saviors in our society, find themselves with better quality of life once they start meditating. The atmosphere around them just improves. There is even a study showing the improved quality of life for nurses.

10. *It all adds up to . . . more money.*

Add up all the other reasons. Your employees stay on the job, and they're happy. They don't get sick as often as before the TM® technique came on the scene. The atmosphere in the company is light, pleasant, and encouraging. Both employees and managers are clear-headed, compatible with one another, and—best of all—creative. People work hard and creatively, in a kind of frictionless flow. People perform well with what they can control, and collective coherence in the company takes care of the things they cannot. Success comes easily, as do profits.

The TM® technique has sneaked into business and into entire companies. It's the impossible fix for collapsing companies just as it is for collapsing people. It's a great fix for companies that are already healthy, too. Some people measure their success in fame rather than money, and the TM® program delivers there, too.*

---

* Portions of this chapter appeared in the online publication Enjoy TM® News in an article titled "10 Reasons Every Business Needs *TM*" by this author, James G. Meade, PhD.

CHAPTER 18

Achieving Fame . . . Lasting Fame.

"After producing over six hundred *Star Trek* episodes and four motion pictures, I guess I'm pretty familiar with stress and anxiety. When I decided to look into TM®, I attended the introductory program at the Encino, California facility. What made me stick around and follow through, was not only my fascination and attraction to the principles of TM®. It was equally a result of the remarkably warm, patient, and informative leadership of Jim and Nina Meade. Their ability to explain the process, and answer myriad questions, made my introduction to TM® both relaxed and confident. The fact that I'm still practicing almost three years later, is a testament to the two directors who taught me the process and gave me the confidence to stick with it."

Star Trek Producer, RICK BERMAN

Not referring to Mr. Berman, but to Hollywood people in general, you'd likely be surprised at how burned-out people can become from working in the film business. I learned about this because they come to me to learn the TM® program. Hollywood is so wildly, cruelly competitive that a simple quieting technique (not TM®) might have a chance, but most people wouldn't have time to do it very often. Besides, they'd be bored. But an enlivening technique, sharpening creativity, giving an experience of heavenly delight . . . they might make time for this sometimes and would of course fully enjoy the tranquility it brings.

Apparently, Disney isn't the dream world you'd expect from seeing its delightful, fun, escapist cartoons. Mickey Mouse. Donald Duck. Snow White. *The Lion King. Beauty and the Beast. Fantasia.* How wonderful—and for generation after generation. Unfortunately, the graphics masters themselves who make those films are sometimes on the edge of despair. One of my favorite private fantasies is to teach the TM® technique to the whole animation staff of Disney. Then the lives of those creating the fantasies could become as beautiful as their fantasies. It doesn't necessarily take "a tough person to make a tender movie" (referring to Purdue's great commercial about how it takes a tough guy to make a tender chicken), but right now I hear that some of those dream-makers are living in a stressful environment. We're talking about a challenging environment being "stressful" if we want to revert to defining stress as something that happens from the outside (and we might as well because our definition of stress as being in our physiology just floats unacknowledged over almost everyone's head).

Anxiety permeates the film industry. It's a life of highs and lows for the participants, especially those in front of the camera. One day you're working and rolling in wealth; the next day you're unemployed and scrambling for it. You can feel desperate, and it often seems you come to an introductory talk on the TM® technique and request to start the program as an unemployed person even though you've been in the "over $200,000" (highest) class for most of your career. Gosh, I'd need some permissions before using the names of some of these household names who come in when they're caught in the inevitable downward cycle. I remember one fellow who felt he was too broke to start. He was paying alimony and child support and house payments and owned a luxury car but was between films. Rich but not rich. Poor even. Producers are under the gun on the set, and they're under the gun when they're out of work. No wonder they can start to unravel. TM® offsets all that disappointment, doubt, and challenge.

"You Got a Problem with That?"

Let's look at some of the famous celebrities in the film industry who have ridden the crest of the TM® technique wave for their entire careers. Clint Eastwood is one. He's been meditating for close to 50 years now. Does anybody call Clint a wuss? Do they call him a "New Ager?" Do they say that Dirty Harry is a closet anything? There is a clip on YouTube of Clint on the Merv Griffin Show in 1978 with Maharishi, the founder of the TM® technique. Clint had to take time off from the set to be on the show, but being with Maharishi meant a lot to him. Merv quips that he lately had a lot of trouble reaching Clint. When he called his house, someone would answer to say sorry, but Clint was unavailable because he was doing his TM—whatever that was.

A producer, director, actor, and composer like Mr. Eastwood is hardly doing his TM® program as a tranquilizer. I mean, sure, it gives him a little respite from his job pressures before he picks up his guns and goes back to shooting people on camera. But what does all that brain coherence mean for a working creative person? It means creativity and focus or, as I like to say, "chilling out while running hot."

Eastwood's output is so staggering that you'd think his biography is fictionalized if it didn't come from a reliable source. He's contributed to more than 50 films and directed over 30. He acts in them, too. of course. And he has earned lots of Academy Award nominations and some wins, even a Best Picture for the 2004 movie "Million Dollar Baby" and for a couple of other movies, too. Most amazing to me is how his productivity continues year after year, picture after picture, award after award. The man is 90. Enough already. My gosh. Shouldn't he be in assisted living? But there he is, standing up to tough guys on camera and coming out on top.

His biographical material says that he hates telling anyone else how to live, and that may be why we don't see him often coming out to tell people to do the TM® technique, although he readily says he does it himself. He is a person who demonstrates how the TM® technique becomes an integral part of a person's life. It enlivens our health and the brain as well as alleviating the stresses and strains of the hard work. It heightens resilience. So now at the age of 90, Dirty Harry is still producing, acting, and directing at a breathtaking pace. His dynamism is unparalleled.

If you wanted to talk about unparalleled creativity, however, you'd have trouble coming up with a better example than Hollywood producer David Lynch. Film students, official and unofficial, look to Mr. Lynch as their ideal. He wrote, directed, and produced the film *Eraser Head,* directed *The Elephant Man,* wrote and directed *Blue Velvet, Mulholland Drive, and Twin Peaks.* Like Eastwood, Lynch displays a range of creativity that can test your credulity. As Wikipedia says, Lynch is a "painter, musician, singer, sound designer, photographer, and actor."

He also inspired and administers the David Lynch Foundation for bringing the TM® technique to schools, to the homeless, to Veterans with PTSD, and to whomever he can connect with who seems to need it. If you wanted to find a completely stellar example of someone whose creativity is not the least stifled by his practice of the TM® technique (and I do want to do just that), you'd be hard pressed to find a more convincing example than the overflowing-with-unbounded-creativity, Mr. David Keith Lynch. Particularly early in his career, when his first film was *Six Men Getting Sick (Six Times)*, he was no doubt an excellent candidate for the benefits of the TM® technique. But now he is legendary for doing an advanced TM® program and never missing a session of the TM® program no matter how inundated with work he may be on the set. That is, his creativity soars after his practice of the TM® technique. It wakes up his brain, and what a brain it turns out to be!

"Giddyup 409"

Another Hollywood type who hardly fits any picture of the shrinking violet is Mike Love, world-beloved founder of The Beach Boys along with his cousin and rival Brian Wilson. At age 80, Love continues every year to go on a road tour that any normal person would find exhausting if not downright overwhelming—one day Birmingham, the next day Auburn, the next Tallahassee and sometimes faraway places like Stockholm. He spends time in the studio to produce the next album. He does composing, mixing the oldies ("Good Vibrations") with the not-quite-so old ("Kokomo") with a steady stream of new songs. (The album *Just Rock* was released two days before I composed these lines.)

According to Wikipedia, "The group has released 30 studio albums, eight live albums, 55 compilation albums, and 71 singles." If that was all you did, it would be enough. Try doing that while being in Tallahassee one evening, packing up at 1:00 a.m. to travel to Norfolk the next evening, and squeezing in a special private concert before your event the next night in Birmingham. If he flies commercial, he sure earns a lot of frequent flier miles.

As upfront as Lynch in his endorsement of the TM® technique, Love in fact is a teacher of the Transcendental Meditation® program who attended teacher training once with the Beatles in Rishikesh in 1968 and again in Mallorca with me in 1972, where he completed his training. Anxiety? Well, he certainly gets the benefits that the TM® technique provides for this, but his main interests are stamina, creativity, stage presence, showmanship, good health, and the old standby of coherent brain functioning. And it has been demonstrated that long-term TM® meditators, defined as of five years or more of practicing meditation, retain their youthfulness when their chronological age is compared to their "biological age," as shown in figure 18.1.

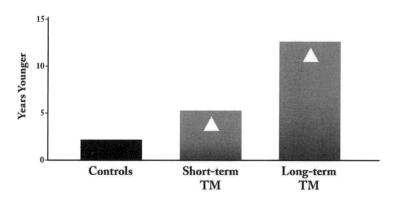

Long-Term TM Meditators
Reduce Their Biological Age

Reference: Wallace, R.K., M. Dillbeck, E. Jacobe, and B. Harrington. "The Effects of the Transcendental Meditation and Tm-Sidhi Program on the Aging Process," *International Journal of Neuroscience* 16 (1982): 53–58.

Figure 18.1 The TM® Meditators look, act, and test out younger than those who do not practice the TM® technique.

Probably, as I think about it, "higher consciousness" tops Mike Love's list of reasons for doing the TM® technique, though he has told me that he uses the practice to maintain his grueling schedule. Nevertheless, "running hot" is at least as big a benefit of the TM® program as chilling out, and both happen simultaneously for these larger-than-life entertainment figures.

Stern, Seinfeld, Brand, and More

How about Howard Stern? I realize this discussion seems skewed toward the manly types, never to be thought of as pushovers or sissies, but that's just the way it is coming out. The TM® program may seriously disable worrying, but it does not, it would appear, do anything to weaken the effect of testosterone in our human body. As a teacher of the TM® program, I hear often how Stern gave the recommendation that brought a candidate in to learn. A radio personality with his show *The Howard Stern Show*, Mr. Stern does not shy away from controversial topics and discussions of sexual matters, and he draws large audiences not only from the wide interest in these subjects but from his lasting and endearing interviews delving into them. "Chilling out?" Of course. But "running hot" is his story, and if the TM® technique strengthens both, then he is indeed a prime example.

Do you like your stand-up routines edgy and fearless? Do some Russell Brand. What about Jerry Seinfeld? Does the TM® technique make him funnier? During his long-running TV show or doing stand-up around the world, he has to draw upon an ever-renewing reservoir of inner creativity. So do Ellen DeGeneres, Oprah, Scorsese, Cameron Diaz, and Katy Perry. (There's a warrior. Check out her song "Roar.")

Think about what Stephanopoulos, Soledad O'Brien, and Hugh Jackman have accomplished. Or one of my heroes of my youth, Joe Namath. He was quoted in his hometown newspaper, *The Beaver County Times* of Beaver, PA, saying that he started the TM® program in his playing days and "I gave it a try and immediately loved it. To this day, I use my mantra daily."

If you are wondering about young stars who do TM®, there are lots more besides Katy Perry and Russell Brand and Cameron Diaz. Moby is a TMer. According to the media website thrillist. com, others also enjoying daily transcending are Aziz Ansari, Gisele Bündchen, Lykke Li, Jennifer Aniston, Kate Hudson, and Gwyneth Paltrow. Some YouTube stars have made their way to the practice of TM®, including Robby Hauldren of the band Louis the Child, and from cable channels like Bravo we have the likes of rising stars Julie Goldman and Brandy Howard from *The People's Couch*. Many others from streaming TV sharpen their skills and relieve their stress with TM®, including Netflix actor Marielle Scott. I taught a ballplayer the other day, and he said I could add his name: Marcus Stroman of the Chicago Cubs.

If you thought the TM® technique could make you enterprising and versatile and strong and irrepressible and creative as this catalog of people from Eastwood to Moby, you would never again think of the TM® technique as *only* a sedative, as only a chill-out means with the concomitant risks. Hardly. It lights you up from the inside. Would it not only relieve your stress but possibly turn you into a high-performance wonder like the people in these pages? Why not? The TM® technique is chill out and heat up—all of which reinforces the point that, actually, relieving anxiety is just a tiny part of what the TM® program is about.

And here's another area of surprising TM® results. When you stop and think about what the TM® program is designed for, it's quite breathtaking. It does routinely accomplish what seems impossible. And something truly challenging is breaking addiction. You know how nearly impossible it is to conquer addiction. When you hear that someone has gone to rehab the next thought is usually, "And how many times now have you been to rehab?" Addictions are tough to kick.

CHAPTER 19

Inescapable Addiction: A Way Out

"When I was 26 years old I started to smoke weed and some other different drugs. . . . Bit by bit my weed usage increased. I couldn't do and didn't want to do anything without it even when I was 40. Jim and TM® saved my life. Two days after first meditating I had no urge in me to stay high anymore. Meditation gave me this pure joy and calmness that I was looking for all of these years. Since then I've had weed around me from friends on occasion, and I never had even a little urge to go back to it. All I need is my 20 minutes of peaceful time twice a day to fulfill my life."

T. O.

The TM® technique heightens performance. People who practice the TM® technique often attract money. They get better jobs or leave their jobs to follow their dreams (which materialize). The TM® technique is not just a tranquilizer. Here is another notch in its belt. It frees us from addictions. We all have our compulsions. Our cravings. They're annoying, sometimes costly, definitely distracting, sometimes self-destructive. The TM® technique helps with them, and there's research on that, too. As for anxiety, well, control those raging addictions, and we have one less thing to worry about.

Cigarettes, Alcohol, Pot, Pills

Addiction can be a real problem for worried people, for sure. What do you do when you're miserable? Drink. Smoke. Sniff. Eat. Shop. Watch porn. Pop a pill. Cram things into your mouth or into your mind to try to take you out of the funk you're in. The TM® technique, conveniently, doesn't just calm you down. It actually helps to fight addiction.

Figure 19.1 shows that the TM® technique helps people to overcome addiction to cigarettes more than other methods of treatment. Whatever

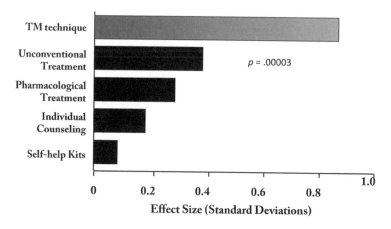

Effectiveness in Decreasing Cigarette Use
Meta-Analysis of 131 Studies

Reference: *Alcohol Treatment Quarterly* 11: 13–88.

Figure 19.1 The TM® technique helps fight that urge for "just one cigarette, just one puff."

other treatment method is chosen rather than the TM® technique, the participants tend to stop over time and they also find the treatment becomes less effective. A study found that TM® participants keep up their TM® practice, and the TM® technique works better and better against addiction over time. In some cases, for example, people do not just find that they do not want a cigarette. They find the thought of a cigarette downright repugnant.

Diving Deep, Not Just Talking

Studies also show that practicing the TM® technique reduces alcohol use. Let's look at that. I can't tell you how many times I've heard people tell me about it once they start the TM® technique. "I was at a New Year's Eve party a week ago," a woman told me, "and when they passed the drinks, I left mine sitting on the tray. I just didn't want it. I didn't even know why. I just didn't." There are lots of reasons, even biochemical reasons, why the desire for alcohol decreases. People attest that the TM® technique can increase their willpower for stopping drinking. Many studies have indicated that the desire decreases more from the use of the TM® technique than from standard prevention programs (including the use of peer influence, which is pretty strong in Alcoholics Anonymous and definitely plays a role in giving up drinking—much more than from "preventive education.") After all, addicts know they should not drink, and they understand why. But the education does not negate that strong compulsion to have just one more drink.

Likewise for drug users, including addiction to prescription drugs, the TM® technique is not only effective; it is more effective than other treatments. Interesting, too, is the discovery that the TM® technique has a stronger effect on discouraging drinking for serious users of alcohol than for more casual drinkers, just as the TM® technique has a bigger effect for those with extreme anxiety than for those with lesser levels of anxiety. If you light a match in a sunny room, you do not even see it. Light that match in a completely dark room, and it is blindingly bright. It is the same with alcohol addiction.

Other research has shown that because the beneficial effect of the meditation on the addict's mind emerges from a deep level of consciousness, the change for those practicing the TM® technique is a lasting change.

Hormones. It's Hormones.

What is going on inside when people find themselves simply not desiring the alcohol or drug or cigarette or other addictive substance any longer? We talked earlier about the stress Roto-Rooter aspect of the TM® technique. Stress is physical, and the practice of TM® allows the body to run a clean-up campaign against its own stress. Scientists have concluded that, thanks to the profound yet energizing practice of the TM® technique, the hormones that drive us into addictions decrease, and serotonin (which takes away that desire for self-medicating) increases. See figure 19.2.

Neuroendocrine Mechanism of Recovery from Drug Use
The Virtuous Cycle by which TM Reduces and Prevents Drug Abuse

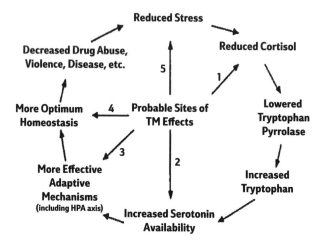

During TM, (1) cortisol decreases by 30% , which reduces baseline cortisol by 30-40% during the day and night. This results in (2) increased serotonin levels, and (3) more effective responses to challenges, with more rapid recovery from stressful episodes, which (4) maintains a more optimal homeostasis as indicated by lower resting levels of heart rate, respiratory rate, etc. One experiences (5) greater success in life, less anger, increased equanimity, and greater happiness, thus eliminating the desire to take drugs and alcohol.

Figure 19.2 The virtuous cycle. How the TM® technique reduces and prevents drug use.[10]

Study researchers Walton and Levitsky have proposed first a "vicious cycle" and then a virtuous cycle brought on by the TM® program. The two researchers have proposed a neuroendocrine mechanism for how chronic stress creates a vicious cycle of biochemical events, which leads to increased drug and alcohol abuse as well as to violence and disease. In their model, chronic stress elevates cortisol, which, through biochemical mechanisms, results in decreased serotonin availability. Reduced serotonin results in less effective adaptive mechanisms, such as the inability to respond effectively to challenges and slower recovery from stressors. That inability results in suboptimal homeostasis, which is experienced as feelings of depression, feelings of anxiety, feelings of being unable to cope, and helplessness.

Substance use is a behavioral attempt to restore the system to a more optimal state. When people feel depressed, they take an upper; when overly anxious and agitated, they take a downer. When feeling bored, insignificant, or trapped in a situation they cannot cope with, they may take alcohol or a mind-altering drug. In this view, all of substance abuse is fundamentally an attempt to restore the system to a more ideal state. If there could be a way to normalize the system naturally, then that would undermine the neuroendocrine motivation to take drugs. Walton and Levitsky document the evidence of how TM® addresses the vicious cycle of drug abuse on several levels.

In brief, the stress hormone (cortisol) goes down (hallelujah), and simultaneously the happiness and evenness hormone (serotonin) goes up. Given that drug and alcohol use tend to make the TM® technique less effective, who wants to make the choice to give up the meditation practice that is working so well to return to an addiction that is just flat-out harmful to the body? TM® breaks the vicious cycle and brings on the "virtuous cycle" where the benefits of a complex chain of events reinforce themselves through feedback loops to end in favorable results.

No More Coffee Shakes

Some TMers know from experience that their addictions mysteriously drop off or slide under control. Following are a few reasons for that:

1. People love the lightness, easiness, and cleanliness they feel in the body from practicing the TM® technique. They just don't want to mess that up. It's a real thing. Cigarettes have always given them a headache, but now they're sensitive to that. Coffee has given them the shakes, or, you know, some jitters, but they craved it. Now they don't think it is worth getting these side effects.

2. Their brain is less stressed thanks to the transcending. In their clarity, they can more readily resist temptation. They

can see a little balance sheet of the pros and cons of that next drink or the toke on the reefer or the little shopping trip on the Amazon Prime website or that hot dog with all the fixin's. They can say "no" more readily than before, not necessarily easily and not every time, but they see their brain power begin to kick in.

3. Meditators don't want to sacrifice even a single brain cell. Even just from having the experience of transcending, people sometimes want to create the optimum grounds for the transcending to happen again. It's bliss. It's love. It's oneness with the universe. It's salvation. It's a natural high. Sometimes, I'm just sayin', people don't want to risk jeopardizing it. Really. They've told me so.

4. Sometimes they're aiming for the natural, all-time, unshakable high, the ultimate endless nirvana. With no side effects. People who take substances are looking for relief from anxiety, sure, but they want to escape from the persistent boundaries of a daily life that, let's face it, tends to be humdrum and not satisfying and even downright boring. I mean, all right is okay, I suppose, but we're not on this spinning billiard ball (the Earth) just to be all right day after day. We want *it*. We want it all, and we want it now. That all comes with living inside that field of the transcendent, only living it all the time. People want that sometimes. Who can blame them?

The fight against addiction, we can say, is just a fringe benefit of the TM® technique. Addiction clinics could make the TM® technique their go-to solution for addiction, and they should. But they don't. Addicts mostly don't either. A lot of the time addicts are just too brain-blocked to listen to much of anything, let alone something so sweet-sounding and abstract as the Transcendental Meditation® program. One time a professed addict who had learned TM® brought in a dozen or so fellow addicts from her rehab center. We gave them the pitch on the TM®

technique as the solution to addiction. As I recall, none of them "started" TM®. They weren't motivated the way those desperate people in our opening chapter were motivated, even though you'd think they would be. They didn't begin the program, which is usually the case whenever we give a talk to any group other than the ones who have trickled in because they are stressed out and know they need help or, as seems to be a trend, are sincerely motivated to gain higher consciousness.

I think about the things these people with addiction problems may have missed out on. Lower blood pressure. Fewer deaths from heart disease. A stronger immune system. Fewer hospital admissions. A solution to their addiction. And another big one—increased youthfulness, the long-sought fountain of youth.

CHAPTER 20

Hey, Ponce, That Fountain You Wanted . . .

"Our quest in the field of health and life is for immortality."

"The basis of continuity of life is in that quality of physiology which will not be subject to wear and tear during its performance."

MAHARISHI MAHESH YOGI

Fixing anxiety. You'd think that would be enough to convince us of the merits of the TM® technique, and for anxiety sufferers it certainly seems like enough when they are in the throes of their nervous stomachs, jitters, and overall fear. Getting stress out of the way and connecting with the inner field of pure consciousness can also increase our odds of fame, fortune, and freedom from addiction. Here's another benefit, too: finding the long-sought fountain of youth. The fountain is not in Florida, as Ponce de Leon may have hoped. We have a new candidate for its source—our overflowing bliss in the field of pure consciousness inside.

Creases Soften Right Away

Going anecdotal is not enough for such a crucial question: "Is there a way to increase our life span and our enjoyment of life as it extends?" Too bad we cannot rely on our unscientific observations, because what we see is quite remarkable. When people come to learn the TM® technique, the creases in their faces soften right away, and they look younger. Beautiful women look strikingly more beautiful. People should think of centers for teaching the TM® technique the way they think of nail salons, beauty parlors, and clothing shops—oh, and gyms and yoga studios. The TM® technique seems, anecdotally, to make us appear younger.

One day I was visiting a friend at his company (a friend made wealthy by the way the TM® technique prepared him for business and enjoying a measure of fame through his publications). "I liked your brother," I said of his visiting relative. "He must be an older brother." "Actually," the friend said of his nonmeditating sibling, "he's younger." But he looked older. He had lines in his face. He did not seem happy.

Turning to our recent examples from previous chapters, we can speak again of Clint Eastwood. He is not in his later years the gun-toting Josey Wales, his role in 1976 when he was 45, or Dirty Harry as he plays him in later movies, but even the much older Walt Kowalski in *Gran Torino* (2008) can handle himself when it comes to a fight.

Mike Love and David Lynch remained creative and productive well beyond the norm, and others like Tom Hanks and Seinfeld joined in. Whether intentionally or not they may have been aided in part by the TM® technique to prolong their careers and youthfulness as they performed. And consider Susan Sarandon, who keeps popping up in movies and TV shows long after you would think her age had caught up with her. She starred in *Ride the Eagle* that came out in 2021 and the movie *Blackbird* that was new on Netflix in 2021. Around the time this book is published we can see her in Fox TV's musical drama series *Monarch* playing the "Queen of Country." Rupert Murdoch managed to scrape together the course fee and in 2013 at age 82 began the transcending practice that appears to maintain youthfulness into the later years.

Watch, out Aging. Here comes the TM® technique

As is the case with so much else with the TM® technique, scientists have tested the validity of many reports of seemingly impossible reversal of aging. As the official chart from the TM® program explains beneath these results, "The physiological and psychological changes that result from the TM® practice are opposite to the changes caused by aging, which means that much of the wear and tear to the system caused by aging and stress can be slowed, and even reversed, through the very deep rest of the TM® technique."

Choose your favorites from the figure 20.1 chart. Blood pressure, researched thoroughly, goes up with aging and down with the TM® technique. And cholesterol. There's another one that goes up with aging, as

Reversal of Aging Process
Through the Transcendental Meditation Technique

PHYSIOLOGY	Through aging	Through TM	PSYCHOLOGICAL	Through aging	Through TM
Blood pressure	⬆	⬇	Susceptibility to stress	⬆	⬇
Auditory threshold	⬆	⬇	Behavioral rigidity	⬆	⬇
Near-point vision	⬆	⬇	Learning ability	⬇	⬆
Cardiovascular efficiency	⬇	⬆	Memory	⬇	⬆
Cerebral blood flow	⬇	⬆	Creativity	⬇	⬆
Homeostatic recovery	⬇	⬆	Intelligence	⬇	⬆

BIOCHEMISTRY			HEALTH		
Cholesterol concentration	⬆	⬇	Cardiovascular disease	⬆	⬇
Hemoglobin concentration	⬇	⬆	Hypertension	⬆	⬇
			Asthma (severity)	⬆	⬇
			Insomnia	⬆	⬇
MIND-BODY COORDINATION			Depression	⬆	⬇
Reaction time	⬇	⬆	Immune system efficiency	⬇	⬆
Sensory-motor performance	⬇	⬆	Quality of sleep	⬇	⬆

⬆ measures that go up   ⬇ measures that go down

Figure 20.1 Measures that go up and down with aging and improve through the practice of TM.

we all know. And it's been shown to go down with the TM® technique. As far as learning ability, we all know about old dogs. Maybe they can't learn new tricks not because they're stubborn but because their brains are getting foggy. The TM® technique comes to the rescue because it increases learning ability. And heart disease? It goes up with aging and down with the TM® technique.

Figure 20.2 charts a study backing up the finding of increased cognitive ability in the elderly. (I mean, I'm not saying the ability goes back to their peak times in their teens, but it goes up.) And it goes up more if you transcend than if you use techniques where you do not dive inside. Figure 20.2 shows what the TM® technique can do compared to alternative choices.

Stress is the culprit. It ages us. In graduate school in literature courses I studied the illustrated poetry of the great William Blake, whom you probably know best from the line of verse "To see a world

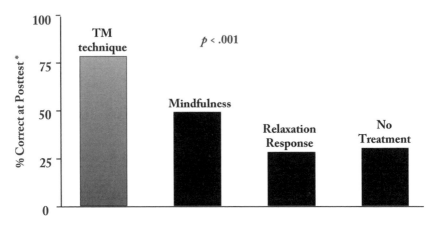

Improved Cognitive Flexibility in the Elderly
Through the Transcendental Meditation Technique

A study of 80-year olds conducted at Harvard found that practice of the Transcendental Meditation Technique increases cognitive flexibility.

Reference: *Journal of Personality and Social Psychology* 57, no. 6 (1989): 950–64.

Figure 20.2 Thinking gets more flexible for people who do the TM® technique.

in a grain of sand," although I like him especially for saying, "If the doors of perception were cleansed everything would appear to man as it is, Infinite." If you look at William Blake's *Songs of Experience*, old people are all bent over. They are hooded, wearing cowls with a long cloak. He shows them as stressed out. "The facts are in: stress ages you prematurely," reports researcher on aging and author Dr. Robert Schneider. As we have discussed, the TM® technique is the stress pump. Ridding us of stress, it is clearing out the cause of aging.

Those Who Practice the TM® Technique Live Longer

So, let's get to the heart of the matter here. Maybe you stay younger with the TM® technique, but do you live longer? A study led by that same Dr. Schneider affirms that indeed we do live longer with the TM® technique. Figure 20.3 gives the statistics.

Reduced Mortality

Through the Transcendental Meditation Technique

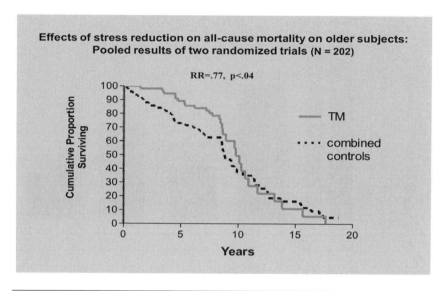

Figure 20.3 Older people who do the TM® technique live longer than those who do not. [11]

And, perhaps not surprisingly as we think of the relative power of various mental techniques, research affirms that the TM® technique increases longevity more than mindfulness and other rival practices as shown in figure 20.4.

Schneider, too, has been the lead researcher on studies of heart disease. His classic study showed the TM® technique to decrease the risk of subsequent heart attacks by 50 percent, as shown in chapter 13. It decreases the risk of congestive heart failure, of angina pectoris, and of heart attacks, strokes, and (the biggie) death. The TM® technique battles hardening of the arteries. A study has even found that the TM® technique helps fight against another risk factor in heart disease— enlargement of the left ventrical (the one that does the heaviest pumping) as I discussed in chapter 13.

Here's another one about aging. The people practicing the TM® technique are happier than non-TMers. I don't mean to be confrontational

Increased Longevity
Through the Transcendental Meditation Technique

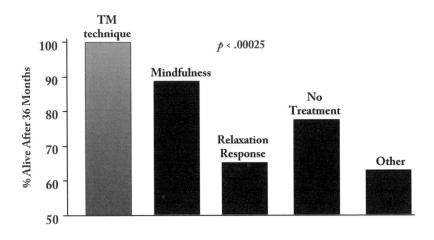

Figure 20.4 Those doing the TM® technique outlive people who rely on other practices.[12]

or dismissive. But there is research showing improved quality of life in old folks, which I am correlating with happiness. Quality of life means a lot of things, but most of them originate on the inside. One study looked at self-actualization in the elderly, that condition known as being inside your skin or comfortable with your self or, as I like to say, happy. That research found that the TMers were two to three times more self-actualized than people doing other relaxation techniques or other meditations.

Even better, elderly folks meditating with the TM® technique don't feel as old as, like, your run-of-the-mill old folks or even old folks doing other meditation practices as shown in figure 20.5. Hey, if you don't feel it, you are not it. You are not as old. With all that we know about the overall effects of the TM® technique, you probably have fewer aches and pains, less disturbing signals coming from your chest, better quality of sleep at night—the whole ball of wax.

The TM® technique does not operate on the surface, as we've been saying. The game of remaining young is played, above all, at the level

Feeling Less Old When Elderly
Through the Transcendental Meditation Technique

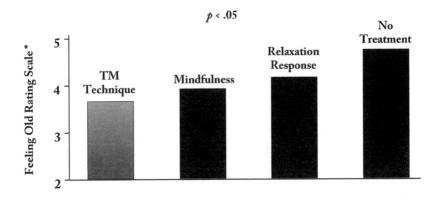

Figure 20.5 Oldsters doing the TM® technique don't feel so old.[13]

of the DNA. Epigenetics, the study of how our behavior and and environment can cause changes "on top" of our genes, is replacing genetics in determining our health and how long we live. We have learned that life style, such as what we eat and how active we are, affects how our genes work and can be more important than our genetic constitution in keeping us young. The Transcendental Meditation® technique does result in improved "gene expression." In other words, changes happen at the almost deepest level, DNA expression. Some of those changes reported in figure 20.5, our chart of aging, are happening at the level of gene expression.

What about the big bugaboos as we age, dementia and Alzheimer's. The TM® technique is not the complete stopper there that we would like. It helps, certainly, and it helps manage the stress and anxiety we experience as we go through such a major decline in brain power. UCLA researcher Dr. Dale Bredesen, author of *The End of Alzheimer's: The First Program to Prevent and Reverse Cognitive Decline*, says "You want to lower stress. Again this is where things like TM come in to be so helpful."

Improved Memory in the Elderly

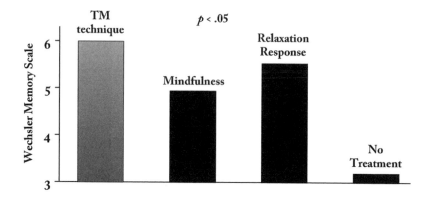

A study of 80-year olds conducted at Harvard found that practice of the Transcendental Meditation technique increases the ability to memorize new material.

Reference: *Journal of Personality and Social Psychology* 57, no. 6 (1989): 950–64.

Figure 20.6 The TM® technique helps memory in the elderly.

What about memory itself? Does the TM® technique help with memory as we age? Will it keep us from forgetting our keys, losing our glasses, not being sure what we started out to do? I'm not saying it might give us a photographic memory or anything like that. But the research says that the TM® technique helps our memory. See figure 20.6.

Telomeres Don't Lie

Here's one of the best ways to tell if you are aging or not, better than how many lines you have in your face or how creaky your joints have become. Telomeres, which are protein caps on the ends of your chromosomes. Again, we are looking at effects at the genetic level. Aging shortens those telomeres, and so does stress. The TM® technique helps us keep them long. Scientists these days, who solve crimes using genetic evidence instead of fingerprints, can test the lengths of our telomeres. Figure 20.7 shows a study of the effects of the TM® technique on telomerase (sometimes dubbed "the immortality enzyme") responsible for maintaining the length of telomeres.

It would be extreme, of course, to say we have discovered the fountain of youth. That fountain may be inside us, in a field of unbounded consciousness. But with the practice of the TM® technique we are only drawing upon it, not gaining complete immortality or anything. "Hey, Ponce De Leon, over here. It's inside us. This is what you were looking for." The field of pure consciousness is eternal, and that is not just an interesting point of information. The TM® technique does allow us to progressively, day by day, live a little bit more in that field, which means that we maintain some of our youthfulness. Maybe we don't become people like the legendary yogis in the Himalayas performing superhuman feats of longevity. But on the other hand, maybe we do. Perhaps we become yogis like the legendary saints in the forests.

Transcendental Meditation and Health Education: Effects on Telomerase

Gene Expression

Funded by National Institutes of Health

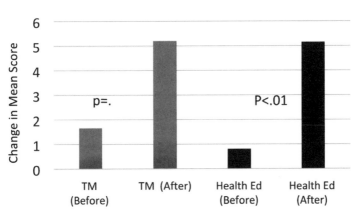

Figure 20.7 The TM® technique helps keep telomeres long for longer.[14]

CHAPTER 21

Becoming an Unintended Yogi

"I was so mad when I started TM®. I felt like a 50-ton whale with so many barnacles on me that I couldn't swim anymore. From the moment I met Jim Meade, his knowledge, joy of teaching and slightly left of center sense of humor started to knock them off. Early on, he mentioned the word 'effortless,' and I thought 'yeah, right.' . . . Now, after several years of his unique brand of "Jimspiration," I can't imagine a day without my two pillars of the TM® technique. I am on track and at peace with my purpose in life. To make people laugh with my heart. Effortlessly. Yeah, right."

CLAY BRAVO, actress, writer, humorista

I didn't want to say this too early in the book, because this book is about anxiety after all, but *fighting anxiety isn't really what the TM® program is for.* Yikes. What? Fighting a tendency to worry is sort of an unintended side effect of the practice. It's an off-label usage with the attendant problems that come with such a thing. What problems? For instance, worry subsides right away and tends to stay away with regular practice. People who began because of anxiety may see no need to be regular in the practice. "Nothing was wrong, so I stopped," one 86-year-old woman said to me when she came to resume her practice of the TM® technique after a long layoff. And she is far from alone.

Of course, there are other effects that can come up, too, when people are seeking a tranquilizer and get cosmic consciousness along the way. If they happen to notice they have changed remarkably, they have to decide what to do with all their new energy (not generally a problem). How about higher consciousness during the day? Generally greater awareness during the day comes on gradually, and people appreciate the calmness and clarity. But they are changing from the way they were before TM®. They don't expect it. Sharp intuition, even superpowers? They're yogis and, well, maybe they weren't planning for all that.

Off-label. Sometimes, when the on-label effects happen, ya gotta decide what to do with all the capabilities when they emerge. In another example, nothing to do with the TM® technique, Viagra is an off-label usage. Researchers at Pfizer were working on a drug to combat hypertension and treat angina (chest pain). I can imagine the scene one day as they worked on it. "This subject still has chest pain, but, boy, he's pretty embarrassed about the other thing going on. Can we reduce this dude's dosage here in the test phase?"

Penicillin, too, is an off-label usage of mold, which was actually just a nuisance and had no formal usage at all in the experiments to develop an antibiotic. The researchers were trying to keep the cultures free of mold, but the mold kept destroying the cultures. Then, eureka! Basically, one day when William Fleming was sorting out his petri dishes filled with staphylococcus, he thought, "Wait a second. We're trying to destroy bacteria, and here's a blob of mold here that is doing just that."

The mold was incidental to their work until somebody shined the spotlight on it and lit it up. Now, boy, do we ever have our antibiotics. We have Amoxicillin/augmentin. Fosfomycin (Monurol), Nitrofurantoin, Trimethoprim/sulfamethoxazole (Bactrim, Septra). A whole huge industry sprang from a few destroyed bacteria cultures in Fleming's lab. Who came up with all those names, and alternative names? The main criterion for naming one must be to make it impossible to remember and even more impossible to spell.

Seeking a Little, Getting It All

Although the off-label uses of a medicine can be valuable in research and medical discovery, they can be risky for consumers, like using the attention deficit hyperactivity disorder (ADHD) drug Adderall to get high when you're not ADHD at all. In the case of the TM® technique, the practice itself is an enlightenment technique that's not likely to be dangerous. The practice is a technique for developing full mental potential or (the only slightly spiritual sounding) "a technique for rising to higher consciousness." The leaders in the movement for teaching the TM® program are easy enough about the misapprehension. You're offering someone a mountain range, and people receiving the lofty peaks talk about it as a small pile of dirt ("great for filling in bare spots in your yard").

In his annual letter to his teachers of the TM® technique, Dr. John Hagelin (the award-winning physicist and head of the TM® technique in the US) recounts the story of Maharishi commenting on the small-scale view Americans were taking of his TM® technique:

> I remember when I started to teach Transcendental Meditation in America, the first article that was written in San Francisco said that this is 'a non-medicinal tranquilizer.'. . . I quite remember that day that I had ALMOST decided to run away, out of that country. (Maharishi laughs.)
>
> I knew that this knowledge was a field of all possibilities in this life, in all future lives, and washed off all the sins of all the past lives, *and* was such a great and universally good-for-all program . . .. But then what kept me in the country was: 'It doesn't matter; even if by mistake someone tastes a drop of nectar, the purpose is done.'
>
> —MAHARISHI
> MERU, Vlodrop, Holland
> January 12, 1995

Now, higher consciousness can sometimes be a tough sell in the pragmatic 2020s. It can sound New Agey to some and to most can sound too abstract and of not enough practical use in everyday life. Does it make money? Does it make you happy? Does anybody really gain it? It can sound academic, frivolous, and—in all too many instances—just meaningless. And that is if people take any interest in the phrase at all, which, basically, they often don't any more than they read poetry or pore over the philosophy of Immanuel Kant. (I can't remember the last time I met a devoted Kant reader. In fact, I never met one. As for poetry, who actually works his/her/their way through the poetry in *The New Yorker* besides me? And I only do it once in a while to prove that I can.)

Still, since we're here, and higher consciousness is on the table, let's take a look at it and see if it relates at all to our exploration of anxiety.

We've said that individuals often have experiences of transcending, and we've made the point that even a single instance of contact with abstract perfection decimates at least some of the stress each of us is harboring.

What, then, is higher consciousness—that is, a sustained transcendence during the day? First of all, people do have experiences of that, too. It's not just for famous people in books like Socrates or Tolstoy. Recently I looked at a roomful of people, say twelve of them or so, when all of them were new meditators. With that particular group, they all felt a certain, new, unusual calmness during the day. It's not true with every group that all will attest to awareness during the day. It's kind of infectious, though. One notes such inner awareness, and others begin to recognize it in themselves. "My kids are a handful, and I'm more patient with them now. They used to get to me, and now they don't." Well, that's lack of anxiety, too, but the point is that some of the inner silence of transcending was still there when their eyes were open.

"Nothing upset me all day," says Jessie, 31 years old and a full-blown millennial cruising through life and extracting the most out of it. She bartends at night and does something with X-Games or something during the day. "It felt so strange that finally I picked a fight with someone just to get back to normality." Higher consciousness is an inner calmness and smoothness that lasts through the day.

Feeling Awake During Sleep. What's Going On?

Higher consciousness can last through the night, too, sometimes causing a bit of confusion or even consternation for those experiencing it. "If I meditate after about 12:00 noon, I can't sleep at night," one Filipino nurse lamented. "Are you refreshed in the morning?" we asked, and she said she was. "Does your husband say you are sleeping?" He did. It turned out that she was maintaining the inner silence, the transcendence, even during sleeping.

In cosmic consciousness, to provide an explanation for the scientific minds in the crowd, the subject in this case displayed the delta brain waves of sleep along with the coherent alpha brain waves of transcending, as demonstrated in figure 21.1. The image is from a presentation by scientist Dr. David Orme-Johnson titled "Enlightenment."

Coexistence of Transcendental Consciousness
With Deep Sleep: EEG Evidence
Through the Transcendental Meditation Technique

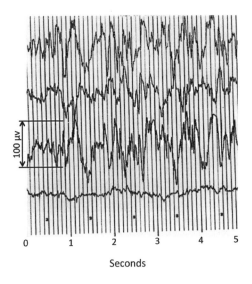

EEG of TC = Moderate EEG, theta/alpha, 10 μv 7-9Hz
EEG of Deep Sleep = Slowest EEG, delta, 100 μv 0-4 Hz
EEG of Cosmic Consciousness = Superposition of theta/alpha on top of delta
Conclusion. This study confirmed Maharishi's prediction that Cosmic Consciousness is a "state in which one lives bliss consciousness, the inner awareness of being, through all the activity of waking and dreaming states and through the silence of the deep sleep state.

Seconds

Reference: *Sleep* 20, no. 2 (1997): 102–110.

Figure 21.1 Theta/Alpha along with Delta brain waves. This indicates awareness during sleep.

Maharishi, the founder of the teaching of the TM® technique in the world, explains the states of consciousness this way: Waking, dreaming, and sleeping are the everyday states that any ordinary person experiences. Transcendental consciousness, measured in coherent alpha waves, is a fourth major state of consciousness. What we're talking about now, in this context, is a fifth major state, Cosmic Consciousness, where we maintain that inner silence all the time outside of meditation—meaning during waking, dreaming, and sleeping.

Experiences of "witnessing" even during sleep, or of broad cosmic awareness during shopping or driving or sitting in class are becoming more and more common among those practicing the Transcendental

Meditation® technique. They are quite enthralling for those who experience them, but often those who practice the TM® technique who do not attend advanced lectures do not know what these experiences are or why they are happening.

"I felt all day as if I was witnessing what was happening," another woman said, a solid citizen who worked a regular job and kept out of trouble. "I was there. I was me. But I was watching a movie as I talked with people or worked on my computer or talked on the phone." I don't think the other people notice that you're "witnessing." Seriously, they don't. You're the same. But you're a yogi in the midst of regular people. You just are.

One woman, another nurse, on her instruction day felt infinitely expanded during her practice of the TM® technique. When she opened her eyes following the meditation practice, she still felt infinitely expanded. Everything on the outside—the room, her chair, the light switch, the woman teaching her the TM® technique, the rug—was infinitely expanded, too. "Inner and outer were the same," she said, starry-eyed and committed to maintaining that experience forever, much like people who have had a glimpse of heaven and simply never want to view anything the same way ever again.

Cosmic consciousness, then, is higher consciousness, and it is the goal of the practice of the Transcendental Meditation® program. It is enlightenment. It is fulfillment of the human condition, complete realization as it is often referred to in the literatures of religions from Islam to Hinduism to Christianity.

In itself, enlightenment is all-time happiness. It is unshakable inner fulfillment. Because you are both infinitely expanded, yet highly focused at the same time, you are maximally effective. Cosmic consciousness is great in a movie producer, for instance. You can juggle the actors and screenwriters and the director and the set designers all at once and not snap unless you want to and not be annoyed at anything or get tired. It's great for an Uber driver as you can start early, run late, fascinate your passengers, not feel perturbed at rude or thoughtless behavior, and feel the whole time as if you are simply the universe expressing itself. It's great for a baseball player, because you don't have to turn to greenies or anything else to pump yourself up during your grueling 162-game schedule. You're in a condition comparable to the famous "zone" all the time, even if for some reason you are not hitting particularly well for a period of time. For a stay-at-home mom, cosmic consciousness is absolutely the cat's pajamas because you can nourish your children endlessly, fulfilling their desires before they even know they have them while preparing sumptuous meals, loving every minute of it, and being a most charming and supportive companion when your husband arrives home (often out of sorts and demanding if he does not share your enlightened state of physiology).

Volumes, endless tomes, exist to extoll the virtues of higher consciousness. Poetry is rife with expressions of it. The best poetry is, in itself, the expanded mind interacting with itself in the spontaneous flow of creation itself unfolding. "Like a long-legged fly upon the stream, his mind moves upon silence," William Butler Yeats says in describing Caesar in his tent. Yeats knows the state of consciousness, I would certainly presume, because his mind is moving the same way. All the great scriptures, particularly their first expressions, are cognitions of nature itself folding back upon itself and emerging in impulses of pure creativity.

Coming back to our prevailing topic, though, we can ask, "What does such a state, however, have to offer the anxiety sufferer with panic attacks?"

Like Inexhaustible Xanax, But Free

If we contort a little bit by acknowledging that people often do not care about higher consciousness but often do care about anxiety, we can point out a couple ways that gaining cosmic consciousness is a boon for people with anxiety and panic attacks.

1. First of all, the inner quietness exists as an immovable, permanent, percolating inner reservoir of the ultimate characteristic of the field of pure consciousness—bliss. Love, too. You can think of it as having an inexhaustible lifetime supply of Xanax, inside, for free. With no side effects, obviously. And with no hangovers and no cravings as you try to get off the substance. Perhaps that would be a good

ad for the Transcendental Meditation® program instead of its current "Evidence-based results." The ad could be, "Try the TM® technique. Like having a lifetime of Xanax inside. Free." The experience, of course, is that those in the throes of misery really can't comprehend such abstraction as Cosmic Consciousness and would "rather just have the pill, thank you very much."

2. Here's a second benefit of cosmic consciousness for someone who, before transcending, was miserable. The higher consciousness from regular practice of the TM® technique is not static but in fact builds on itself. As people practice their 20 minutes twice a day, they keep adding to their already full store of infinite bliss. It churns and plays and delights them in ever-new and exciting ways, showering them with treasures both material and spiritual. And you can hear it now, of course. "Just give me the pill, and I'll think about all your infinite bliss later."

3. How about the fact that the Cosmic Consciousness, for the anxiety sufferer, could be an all-time high? You would be going through day and night floating on a cloud yet performing at virtuoso level. You would be knowing that you are everything, and everything is you, and you are blessed to live fullness eternally as you work as a mail carrier or Amazon help-line person or a Facebook designer. An All-time high? But the sufferer often can't think that way, in cases of extreme stress can barely think at all. So, no.

4. I wonder if "unshakable" would make a difference. I mostly don't think so. Here's a state of life that not only is not depressed or anxious, it is guaranteed *rarely* to be depressed or anxious. If some down mood comes up, it is on the surface while the smoothness prevails at the depths. "Unshakable" pretty much sounds impossible, of course, to those just seeking a little relief.

5. One last try, because all these previous ones sound more or less the same and way too abstract to mean much of anything to someone who thinks she's dying and hasn't slept for weeks. Relief from pain. You see, pain can't coexist with pure consciousness, which is nature in its perfection. People who are transcending find themselves with increasingly less pain. Drastic relief from pain might attract the anxiety sufferer slightly maybe, but he/she/they just wants relief now; permanent or not doesn't matter. "Just give me the pill."

Truly, in fact, the TM® technique for anxiety is an off-label usage of a technique that is for all-time, rapturous fulfillment. Using the TM® technique to fight worry is actually taking a fire hose to put out a candle. It is taking a bulldozer to squash a mosquito (one that is trapped so the bulldozer can't miss her). It is the most astonishing form of overkill. It is wrapping a blanket around your big toe because it has a slight chill. It is forking over a $500 tip to the pizza delivery guy to cover a $20 pizza.

The TM® technique is the all-time solution to everything. Of course it will annihilate your anxiety. You kidding? But, as we say, the application to anxiety—the reason 90 percent of the people I have met come to the practice—is what brings people to the TM® technique, in most cases, not the desire for higher consciousness. This trend these days for people to start the TM® technique because they're desperate for a little peace is some great sleight of hand of the gods. We're miserable, trying everything just for relief, and one of the things we try raises us as close to divinity as the human nervous system can support.

The TM® technique tends to make us happy. Astonishingly, it doesn't *just* make us happy. Even here—oh, no, not again—the everyday and immediately understandable does not really give the picture of what we gain with the TM® technique. What could be beyond happiness? Well, we said that solving anxiety is off-label use of the TM® technique. On-label use is something way sweeter than fixing anxiety, way sweeter than success, way sweeter even than happiness, even than all-time happiness. Let's glance at that "sweeter than happiness," just because it's there and just because it happens for everyone who transcends. Happiness in all its forms is a bit transitory and superficial. The TM® technique is actually for bliss, which in Cosmic Consciousness is permanent and profound.

CHAPTER 22

Looking for Relief, Finding Bliss

"When I came out of meditation and walked through campus, I had one of the most profound experiences in my life. There are really no words that can adequately describe this experience, but I felt like part of a great self-luminous continuum that was walking through itself. Everything had become one silent presence of indescribable beauty, and I was part of that presence, walking through the outer part of me, that was the presence itself. I realize that makes no sense on a logical level, but a feeling of oneness has stayed with me, at least subliminally, throughout my life ever since."

JOHN MEARS, Educator

I don't know if we should get technical here or just stay with the familiar. Here we are, lobbying to convince a world full of miserable people that transcending will end the drought. They don't have to be miserable, we're telling them. They can be on an even keel. "We just want some peace," people keep saying, setting the bar low (at least until they get it), and we're offering them some stability, a respite, just some evenness of mind for a change, a halt in that interminable mental chatter.

We have spoken of Ray Dalio and Clint Eastwood and their dripping-with-wealth ilk. With the Transcendental Meditation® program you don't just chill out. You run hot, by which metaphor we mean that your performance goes through the roof . . . not just up a beat or two, to the second floor or third floor, but through the top. Wall Street, where people measure their wealth in billions, sharpens its performance with the Transcendental Meditation® technique, the self-strengthening practice of kings. And Hollywood, synonymous with dreams fulfilled and living the immeasurably successful life of fairy tales, has made the Transcendental Meditation® program as taught by Maharishi Mahesh Yogi into a widely respected routine.

Happiness, Sure, But That Ain't All

Okay, back to my treasure trove of possibilities here. How about happiness? We can be simple enough about upping the ante. Don't just settle for evenness, for goodness's sake. Don't just settle for tranquility and success. Success rules and sometimes brings with it happiness, but we know that the joy in life can be fleeting or even absent altogether. Heck, you can be an achiever and anxious at the same time. "Even Oprah," as we have said.

The TM® technique provides a continual experience of self-improvement and feeling good. Serotonin, we have pointed out, is the body's natural feel-good drug, and the TM® technique ups our serotonin level. "Enjoy your life and be happy," says Maharishi, here quoted from the website azquotes.com. "Being happy is of the utmost importance. Success in anything is through happiness. More support of nature comes from being happy. Under all circumstances be happy, even if you have to force it a bit to change some long-standing habits. Just think of any negativity that comes to you as a raindrop falling into the ocean of your bliss. You may not always have an ocean of bliss, but think that way anyway and it will help it come. Doubting is not blissful and does not create happiness. Be happy, healthy, and let all that love flow through your heart."

The founder of the TM® program endorses happiness, and experience shows that his technique in fact delivers more than equanimity. It delivers a joyful sail, and you move along on that even keel. I remember the millennial, depressed for years, who soared into happiness once he began the TM® technique and the miserable single mom who found herself dancing around her kitchen and singing after she had been meditating for two days. I enjoy thinking of Denise, previously struggling along in a decent job selling something or other and keeping her head above water, who couldn't stop smiling after she learned the TM® technique. Lois was so happy after her learning that I brought her before the group as exhibit A on her instruction day— just to show them how happy a person becomes in spite of themselves once they learn the TM® technique. Only later did I find out that she suffered from social anxiety, because on that day she was absolutely a paragon of happiness in a social situation.

If we wanted to amplify our argument for the TM® program, then, sure, we could say that the TM® technique makes you happy and not just feeling "smooth," or whatever term you want to use. Serotonin levels could be the mechanics for the transformation, and likely is. But happiness doesn't raise the bar high enough. You don't always have it, even with the TM® technique. People who are always happy are a bit obnoxious anyway. Don't they ever look around them and see how things are? Are they faking it? That all-time happiness is kind of a putdown to the rest of us who are happy sometimes, and just blah sometimes, and also occasionally unhappy. With those always-happy folks we often tend to be kind of, "Would you please go away for a while? I'm happy for you, but please give me a break."

Softer, More Bubbly

Happiness will not do the trick of moving the needle from "my anxiety feels better" to something truly off-the-scale. That something, the ultimate substance (or since it's not manifest, call it a quality), is bliss. Bliss is an innate quality of the fundamental field of life, pure consciousness, the superstring, the unified field. That completely silent field is effervescent in its silence. When we slip into it, even in that very first meditation with a trained teacher and feel ourselves struck with amazement, we are experiencing the true nature of existence—bliss. Bubbling bliss. Percolating bliss. It's just there. We may have lost sight of it in our defeats and disappointments and misery, and we may feel that it is not there *for us* (as if it were a choice and not simply the reality of the unified field), but it is there just as much as the sun is there whether it is obscured by clouds or the spinning of the planet or not. It is still there.

I'm always struck by how Dr. John Hagelin, head of the TM® movement in the US, explained that at the most fundamental level of life, known in physics at times as "the superstring," life consists of little loops like rubber bands. Those loops have spin types. There are five spin types, and they are the building blocks of the universe. Settle down to the finest, purest, most primordial level of life, and it is tiny, spinning loops of energy. "Bliss," in other words.

Neuroscientist Dr. Fred Travis explains in an interview with me that the difference between happiness and bliss is "the difference between changing emotions that give a global evaluation of the situation and the non-changing field of Being that is lived along with the changing emotions." Bliss, not mere happiness, is what we gain when we take on the regular habit of slipping into the absolute twice a day.

"Default Mode Network"

I had the delight of interviewing a scientist from one of the University of California schools. In answering my queries about the nature of bliss, he did in fact take quite a technical route, appropriate for one who is both a medical doctor and a neurologist. He spoke of increased activity in the default mode network (DMN), which is primarily along the midline of the hemispheres of the brain. And he explained that awareness of the external environment is turned off during the TM® technique.

Those are his words, more or less, and they bring the focus to a wonderful thing—the default mode network. In transcending we enliven it, and it is heightened self-awareness (great news for all those seeking to be more self-actualized) and yet there is still what he calls monitoring of the body and emotions. It's what we in the world of the TM® program call "higher consciousness," which is awareness inside and outside at the same time. And now, we're saying as we up the ante in the case for losing anxiety, that we begin to live something that is more stable and permanent than simple happiness (which is good in itself and quite worth having). The most fundamental field of life, the field of pure consciousness, has characteristics—one of which is bliss. As we contact that field regularly in our TM®, we experience bliss during the meditation and also begin to live it in daily life. We begin to live the bliss that is a fundamental characteristic of life but is mostly hidden from us until we find a way to contact it directly.

I spoke with two other scientists about bliss, too. Dr. David Orme-Johnson shared a personal experience with me from an essay he wrote titled "Transparent Darkness:"

Recently I heard that a friend had died after a long period of dementia, which struck me heavily because my father and older brother also died of dementia. I was feeling in a very dark mood during my [meditation] program, grieving and crying. But then I noticed that the grieving was permeated by an underlying glowing bliss that was not touched by the grief. The experience was bittersweet. It is not as if I didn't care. If anything, I am more compassionate and tenderhearted now than ever before.

Never before or since have I had anyone so clearly capture that experience of being blissful inside no matter what, even at times when we are in the throes of misery. The people I met in the room in the first chapter came to an introductory talk about something that might relieve their endless, disturbing mind-chatter, and here is encouragement that they could begin to experience a delicious, scintillating, inner joy even if they still feel miserable on the surface. The bliss just cuts through the misery like a hot knife through margarine, leaving the grief and unhappiness powerless, even if they happen to be still in place, and renders them completely irrelevant. In the clinical sense, the experience is that one simply emerges from depression, which melts away in the presence of bliss.

Only transcending can deliver that experience—bliss amidst misery. It happens, of course, because the default mode network is enlivened, giving us stability and liveliness, whatever is going on in our viscera. Orme-Johnson explains it in technical terms, too:

> In my experience, it is like a tuning fork humming in the background of all activities and experiences that has the quality of unconditional, happy, nourishing well-being, whose presence results in greater waves of appreciation and enjoyment of situational joys like listening to music, eating, nature, etc. Whatever gave joy previously is greatly amplified by it. Experience stirs the quiet, undifferentiated background of bliss into waves of bliss specific to the sensory input stirred by the experience (tastes, sounds, sight, etc.).

Ya gotta love that. More, ya gotta have it. Depression and anxiety and misery disappear, or, even if they don't, they become irrelevant. You're miserable in your bliss, and someone might look on this in confusion because it seems contradictory. Bliss and misery at the same time. You do not live the bliss because of the misery and not in spite of it. You live it along with everything, every emotion and every experience, even, most surprisingly, along with unhappiness.

An All-time Natural High

For those tentative people who meet in my living room week after week, I would love to make the case I have made here. If they would begin the TM® technique, they would not only simply, instantly, put an end to their anxiety (although the end is not always immediate and not always permanent unless they continue to be regular in their practice of the TM® technique). They would experience bliss, that supremely fine quality of the nature of life itself that is simply sublime, that all-time natural high that is what the Creator (if there is one) intended for himself when he expressed himself in mankind.

But, you know, it's enough to let people hope that the TM® technique might numb their agony for a while. That sounds like a lot when you can't get the trembling to stop and you just feel like the world has hemmed you in and won't even let you breathe. But how could anyone imagine experiencing higher consciousness or "bliss" or even hear the words when the reality closing in around them is the feelings of "I can't breathe." "I'm going to die." "Oh, God, I'm miserable." Yeah, I take it back. I guess I shouldn't have brought up all this impossible-sounding stuff. But as we contemplate a little about what's possible, let's look at the world around us these days. Bad news seems to be everywhere. Can this bliss-creating technique bring us any relief on a societal level?

PART V

Afterthoughts

CHAPTER 23

Society Seems Totally Unfixable

"Portland is on pace to surpass its all-time record for homicides this year as its police department is grappling with a surge in gang-related shootings amidst a staffing shortage and continued calls for defunding. . .."

"People are scared. They are angry. They are fed up," Portland Police Sgt. Ken Duilio told the news agency."

Fox News, June 10, 2021

As we survey our world, we have a seriously unmanageable situation on our hands, right? Now, besides everything else, we still have Covid-19 ravaging societies across the world. In the US the vaccine proponents and anti-vaxxers hate each other. Dems hate Republicans, and the aversion is mutual. Some Dems hate some progressive Dems and some hate conservative Dems. The same thing has happened to the extremes within the Republican party. Where do you start to reconcile these raging opposites? Surely not with ideas. People's minds are made up. We all know that.

What are some of our social ills? Internationally, we have war. We have always had war. Our longest war in Afghanistan has drawn to a painful and unsatisfying conclusion. The US, China, Russia, and North Korea are all rattling sabers.

Here in the US, we have recently seen protests that turned violent in LA, Chicago, Portland, and Milwaukee. Race relations is a major concern, and each side is absolutely certain it is right. Gender relations is a hot topic, and reformers are hell-bent to change how we think and react. The Me-Too movement has put everyone on alert. Cancel culture is rampant. If a public figure takes a step, right or wrong, someone is sure to call out, "(S)he should resign." Football coaches face the same. So do tennis players. One confessed recently that the social media treatment she got after she lost the game really disturbed her. She had *lost*, which they knew was what she so deeply wanted to avoid.

Rampant Finger Pointing

Things have gotten so bad in the way we treat each other that sometimes vendors, like a campground I saw recently, put up signs and say, simply, "Be nice," or something like "Be nice or be gone." Often people, in spite of such warnings, are just not good to each other. Finger pointing is so rampant that you get disoriented and you're not sure whom to hate.

We should mention guns. Speak about a lethal center of debate. Gun lovers are fiercely defensive of their right to bear arms. Anti-gunners use a firm logic that if such and such shooter had not had access to a gun, the person would not have been shot. Unfailing logic. Unending debate.

The climate. Oh, my goodness. The sky is falling. No, it really is falling, or at least glaciers and shore lines have been decimated and trees are falling from hurricanes that are the most devastating we have ever seen and forest conflagrations that invite comparison to holocausts. Walls of flame wipe out not only trees and bunny rabbits and coyotes; they destroy environments of our neighbors living in dells that year after year have been quiet and peaceful.

Domestic violence is rife. Some time or another these people loved each other enough to get together, get married, and have children together. But, sometimes, all that gets lost, and their stress breaks out in violence. Spouses suffer. Children suffer and even become orphaned. Yikes.

Have I mentioned crime, which of course should not raise the cry of "Defund the Police" except for those who think that the police are doing the crime, and apparently sometimes they are. Crime has been trending downward for well-nigh 50 years, but Covid-19 brought a spike in criminal behavior. Murders are happening at an alarming rate. Then people go to prison with overcrowded cells and face the flawed court system and the legal dockets.

Everyone seems to agree that we are living in terrible times, except those few, perpetually optimistic souls who are happy and not complaining and manage to enjoy whatever comes. In general, for most, though, life seems a real mess right now. Inflation may bankrupt us all. The absurdly high housing market is likely going to crash. Or not. So could the stock market, of course. Nothing at all is predictable. The advice is to find a nice place to shelter and hope that your home will not wash away in a flood or burn in a fire or become unlivable because of pollution.

Or you could become so mentally deranged that you'll get one of those conditions listed so carefully in *The Diagnostic and Statistical Manual of Mental Disorders* (DSM), which currently lists 297 disorders. In Shakespeare's time, I would surmise the number of these ailments was much smaller—some probably as ordinary as being a little "tetched" or what we call now a bit "touched." But we have made wonderful progress in so many ways.

Blame the President

Whom do we blame? Well, we often start with the president. We might also cast shade on some other elected official, maybe a senator or committee chairman in Congress or a Supreme Court Justice or a governor or mayor or perhaps a business tycoon (yeah, it's all Elon Musk's fault) or an entertainment figure or a sports luminary. (Blame LeBron.) We love to blame, and we love to complain. The simplest thing is to blame the president, and many are relentless about that.

Or maybe the fault is with the press. If you are looking for press you can trust, keep looking, because journalists will unwittingly take off on some wrong tangent from time to time and lead everyone astray. Nobody wants to read in the news that everything is hunky dory, even if it should happen to be. We want calamities and weirdities and disappointment and savagery.

Rarely, I think, do we find ourselves at fault, but one impossibly abstract explanation of our woes places the blame directly there—on ourselves. Sometimes we think of what is happening all around us as our collective destiny. This "karma," I think, is not a cultural concept that has gained much traction with average American families who do not hold Hindu or Buddhist beliefs about the subject. "As ye sow, so shall ye reap." Good luck with having them place much credence on such conceptual thinking.

Who is keeping track of what we do anyway? And how do they enforce it? Even for us as individuals, how do we even know most of the time whether we are doing what's right? Buy a new shirt, and you may be aiding sweat shop conditions in a factory in Vietnam. Walk down the street, and you may be inadvertently encouraging pedestrian activity in a no-pedestrian zone. It is all so complicated that most of us don't think about karma anyway, and in the unlikely event that we did, we would not be able to choose the right actions consistently anyway. Creation is moving, and we can't stand still. Move too fast, and that is bad, too.

So what we have in society is all of us making mistakes. We are messing up, and excuse me for saying so, but you are, too. "Let he who is without sin cast the first stone" seems to have fallen on deaf ears in the world. We cast stones and just figure that "this time, it's them" and let the rocks fly. So be it.

For anxiety, we did finally find a culprit and a way to freedom. Stress is what does it. And we narrowed the definition of stress to something manageable. Stress, we said, is not "out there." It is not situations or emotions. It is "in here." It is tangled and twisted systems in our own bodies. Straighten them out, and the pain and tension and fright just lift.

But this is society we are talking about. Where, exactly, are the twisted and tangled nerves we want to straighten out in society? And, should we find them and straighten them, will that really stop some madman from taking up arms against innocent children or carjacking hapless tourists in Miami? Maybe enlightened crooks will just become more stealthy and effective pickpockets and internet scammers.

If we could lift the stress of society, though, it stands to reason that we would improve the environment around us. If we become enlightened, we'd be really smart, so we could come up with many more good technologies. And when enlightened, we'd accept and adopt those technologies if they were appropriate. Maybe we would stop the oceans from overflowing and the forests from spontaneously combusting and the muggers from mugging. Such happy outcomes happen in the body, we have asserted earlier in this text. You don't have to sort out your own imbalances. You can sometimes make the right adjustments to the body. But when you transcend, the body's intelligence works it out for you. Your digestion improves. You sleep better. And you get through that meeting without having a heart attack. Does the same analysis apply for society as for individuals, namely that we do not have to solve all the outer situations that are stressful (like wars and wildfires and hurricanes) but rather simply Roto-Rooter the stress that is causing those conditions to arise?

Blind Stress-Lowering

Well, the thought is that stress resides in the nervous systems of human beings. If we place those nervous systems in the presence of a field of life that is perfect and lively and transforming, those nervous systems systematically dissolve their stresses. Moving to society, if we dissolve stresses that same way in enough individual people, we expel stress overall from society. In a series of studies in the mid-seventies of the previous century, scientists found that crime and accident rates decreased when as little as one percent of the population in a city was eliminating its stress through regular transcending.

Figure 23.1 gives information about a landmark study by Dr. D.W. Orme-Johnson and others* who tracked the effect of groups of TM® meditators on the war in Lebanon in the 1980s. The notes to the study provide the following explanation of the chart:

> This historic study showed the profound impact on the war in Lebanon of an assembly of advanced meditating experts. During the 60 days of the study, there was a profound correlation between the numbers who gathered to meditate on a

---

* Orme-Johnson, D. W., Alexander, C. N., Davies, J. L., Chandler, H. M., and Larimore, W. E. (1988). "International peace project in the Middle East: The effect of the Maharishi Technology of the Unified Field." *Journal of Conflict Resolution*, 32, Vol. 4 (1988), pages 776–812.

Application to the Middle East
An Historic Case Study

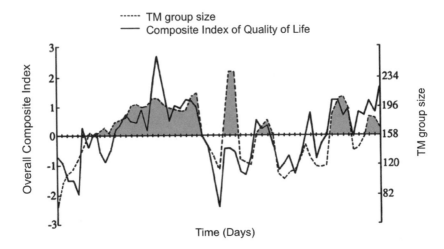

------ TM group size
——— Composite Index of Quality of Life

Reference: *Journal of Conflict Resolution* 32, no. 4 (1988): 776–812.

Figure 23.1 Dissolve stress, fix society.

daily basis and progress towards peace among the warring factions (as measured by daily war deaths, war injuries, levels of conflict [bombs dropped, bullets fired], and negotiated progress among the rival factions).

Here is a way, pretty much blindly, meaning without targeting particular culprits such as muggers or burglars or internet scammers or the president or the Speaker of the House, that we can lower the stress level in society just as we can in individuals. We can lower it significantly. Nobody even needs to know it is happening, although presumably the people who are doing the transcending know that they feel better themselves. They need not have any awareness of their effect on society. They will have the effect anyway.

Will such transcending and concomitant stress release have an effect on the destiny of a community or a nation? That would be the objective and should happen. People who are not under stress are nicer and don't do as many wrong things as they did before their anxiety was alleviated. If their behavior improves, they don't build up a destiny of deserving the terrible consequences of things like forest fires and hurricanes, street crime and school shootings, and general meanness and unhappiness.

Sure, solving our social conflicts can seem impossible. We haven't succeeded very well at it so far, in spite of the endless parade of humans willing and eager to step up as president or another official to take a whack at solving the problem of social unrest. Dissolving stress could be a giant stride toward easing calamitous social problems that seem to come crashing down on us daily. The solution is at hand, not just for our individual anxiety (which lessens almost immediately when we start the TM® technique) but for the broader arena in which we operate, the society around us. Research has demonstrated this.

CHAPTER 24

Why Can't Books Alone Teach You the Transcendental Meditation® Technique?

"I thought I was meditating before. Boy, was I wrong!"

TM® meditator JOSH GRIFFITH, soap opera writer,
after learning the official TM® technique in-person
with a certified instructor.

Let's get down to brass tacks. How do you learn this way of meditation and the calm that comes with it? Learning to dive beneath the surface of life on your own can seem frustrating, even impossible. It's true that you can't learn the technique from a book, not even this one. And it's true that you have to go through formal instruction.

I need to tell you that the whole experience wouldn't work if I tried to teach it to you here. Such teaching from a book would be grossly unfair to you and to me, too.

To give an example of the possibility of falling into the wrong hands when seeking to learn the practice of TM® meditation, I will tell you of a man I met in Jamaica when I was teaching the TM® technique there:

"I do TM®, too" the man told me.

"Where did you learn it?" I asked.

"From my therapist, he replied."

"Is he a certified teacher?"

"He's a psychiatrist."

"Did he do a ceremony before he taught you?"

"No. He didn't need to."

He continued to insist, "I do TM®. Please tell people I am a TM® technique meditator."

Ah, the challenges we face!

First of all, we were having enough problems getting the Jamaicans to be interested in learning the program. We ran into a lot of superstition and mistrust, which can happen anywhere.

If they listened to Renee, they might think they could pick it up in a few minutes from a psychiatrist or almost anyone. This illustrated the problems that can come up when someone has not learned the TM® technique from a certified teacher. Because Renee had not actually learned the real TM® technique, we couldn't meet with him as an equal to make sure his practice was running smoothly. We couldn't invite him in to learn advanced techniques. We couldn't invite him to meetings with those who have learned how to meditate. If a teacher does not have a foundation in the principles we teach, he cannot refine them or add to them.

When you learn about the Transcendental Meditation® program properly from a certified teacher, you begin with the actual experience of going within, not with an emotional mood or an intellectual idea. For example, I have recounted some of the utterances we hear from those first learning. "Wow!" is the most common. People report feeling deeply relaxed. "My arms and legs went numb." "Time disappeared." "I didn't want to open my eyes" and, all the time, they repeat "Thank you" to their teacher. These learners deserve great respect at this significant time in their life and, of course, they deserve to be led by an authentic teacher of Transcendental Meditation.

Passing Along the Experience

There is a whole inner mechanics that explains why you have the experience of transcending, usually for the first time in your life, when you learn in private from a legitimate teacher. It is not the genuine TM® technique if you are learning from a non-teacher or learning from some electronic source like a TV or your computer over Skype or some such thing. The certified TM® teacher, in person, initially invites you to the experience of meditation, and in this special situation you begin to settle in. The teacher whispers some instructions. He or she, based on your response to the experience you are having, whispers further instructions. He or she is always there with you in person. The instructor, he, himself, who is in the habit of transcending, is guiding you.

Often the instruction goes well right away. Sometimes you have questions, and the teacher knows how to give you the experience of transcending. The teacher stays with you to assure that you transcend. If you teach yourself from a book or from a friend who has not been trained, you will not learn the technique properly and would not transcend.

Okay, now let's think about what it is that's being offered to you. You are being handed a solution to a lifetime of anxiety and suffering from problems—possibly all in a single moment. And the solution to anxiety is just a minor add-on to what else you are receiving. You're going to have revised brain functioning, that is, a clarity of thinking in your daily life. That clarity translates into higher performance in your work. You will become "easier" or more relaxed in your relationships and thus more likable so that you get along better with your husband or wife, your in-laws, your crotchety boss, even your dog. (Seriously. People tell me these things. I remember one fellow telling me that his friend's dog, who usually stayed away from him and appeared to dislike him, came up with wagging tail and asked to be petted once the fellow had started the TM® technique.)

You are getting, when you learn the authentic TM® technique, so much in a single package. You're not just receiving simple relaxation. That you can probably get from advice on the internet or from a book or from an app. You can get calmness watching a movie, though I think films don't tend to be particularly ease-making, for the most part. You find yourself on the edge of your seat from the tension, feeling the same highs and lows as the characters in the movie.

When learning the TM® technique properly, you begin to have the experience of transcending. The mind goes from the everyday surface level of consciousness, where you've been performing so far, to finer levels of creation. And the thing about experiencing those levels is that, simply in themselves, they soak your nervous system with upliftment and positivity and creativity. If you don't learn the TM® technique the right way, one-on-one, with a certified instructor, you don't transcend.

You might think you're transcending. You might have a mood of feeling you are diving beneath the surface. The book or voice on your computer or whatever is teaching you might even tell you that you are transcending. But take it from one who did everything to try to transcend before learning the TM® technique the correct way, you almost certainly won't be.

"I Thought I Was Meditating Before This."

If you think you are meditating and even transcending, but are not, you may even convince yourself intellectually that you are meditating in the fullest sense. I remember Josh, who had been, as it were, turning cartwheels in his effort to meditate. When I brought him out of his first session in the actual TM® technique, he said simply, "I thought I was meditating before. Boy, was I wrong!"

The actual instruction is not given in only one day. The teacher meets with you over four consecutive days for a short time and explains what your experience will be after one day and after two days and after three days. You have not officially learned the Transcendental Meditation® technique until you have completed all four days of instruction. Each day of instruction adds essential information. Follow-up sessions are available, too.

Most people come with a preconceived idea of what will happen during their meditation. The preconception is based on a lifelong experience of the waking state of consciousness. They then expect some variation of the waking state because it's all they know. Commonly, they expect to stop thinking. Even if they are expecting bliss or love or inspiration, once they begin the actual Transcendental Meditation® technique they are no longer experiencing their idea of something wonderful but experiencing what really does happen when they go within. It's a lot to absorb.

As I mentioned in the story of Renee, once you have had the four required days of instruction, in person, with a certified teacher, you belong to a worldwide organization. In attending meetings with the organization, you strengthen and refresh your experience. Advanced programs and retreats are available.

We Don't Disappoint People by Offering Weak Instruction

I know sometimes people feel that something is being somehow perversely withheld from them when we don't just casually give them the TM® technique the way you might show someone a yoga posture in your backyard or teach them how to pay attention to the present moment or listen to an expert who will lead them through a guided meditation. But it's the opposite of disappointing them. We are giving them so much more.

When a qualified teacher declines to give you the technique casually in some informal setting, the person really has no choice for the simple reason that he wants you to have this precious, life-altering technique for the ages. He so wants you to have it. To give you some hollow shell of the real technique just leaves you disappointed. A precious moment has passed when you might have begun on the path to fulfillment.

We invite you to come in and learn the right way. Everybody will be happy then—you, especially. I once had a general in Nepal who wanted to learn the TM® technique, a most persuasive and busy Brigadier General. "Just give me the technique," he said on the first day, in the way that people speak who are accustomed to having their orders followed. When he said it, the first words that sprang to the tip of my tongue were the ones he wanted to hear. Giving this man what he wants was the natural behavior in his presence. But, of course, "I can't do that," were the words that came out. You do not let such a precious person come so close to learning and then not have the experience.

"All right," he finally agreed, but he threatened that he would not come on the three required days of follow-up. On the first follow-up day he did show up, and he brought a gift to his teacher, a woolen scarf. The next day, despite the hesitation over whether he would come, he showed up again, and he again showed his gratitude with a gift. And on the final of the four days, chauffeured the way generals are, he arrived bearing yet another gift.

"This is what I have always been looking for," he said. He had the real experience. "This is the fulfillment of the Hinduism I have been following all these years." (To avoid confusion, I need to tell you the TM® technique is not directly related to Hinduism any more than it is to Christianity or Islam or Buddhism. Transcending, brought by the TM® technique, might be the basis of any religion or any other belief system or not part of any system.)

Although the general had been considering retirement from the military in three years or so, he retired almost immediately after this, saying he wanted just one thing—to gain everything possible from the Transcendental Meditation® program and to teach it to others.

Because I taught him properly, his life was transformed. And I had the honor of been trained and certified as a teacher by Maharishi Mahesh Yogi.

CHAPTER 25

Maharishi Mahesh Yogi

"The life of a saint cannot be known by the instances through which it passed."

Ancient proverb often quoted by MAHARISHI

One day, a couple months before his passing in 2008, Maharishi's group of leaders at the time made a video about Maharishi's influence on them. I haven't seen it. But I know that Maharishi's personal presence transformed many lives. Under his guardianship and teachings, people rose to heights beyond their fondest dreams. Maharishi, when he saw the video, said, "I didn't know." He did not comprehend his profound effect on so many people. Who is this almost indescribable man who, as a very trivial, infinitesimal part of his legacy, offered quite an effective antidote to the age-old torment of mankind that is anxiety?

It's Not About Everyday Instances in His Life

First of all, if a man is fully realized, in the sense of his attaining the possibilities of a fully developed human nervous system, we do not know him in the usual way. Such a person would have a mind and body where the finest field of life, pure consciousness, shines through unobstructed. Maharishi spoke of the possibility of living what he called "unity consciousness," where the person experiences inner life as infinite . . . and also outer life as infinite. Two infinites. Two unbounded oceans of consciousness, which, both being infinite consciousness, are one unified consciousness. Unity.

Maharishi was fond of quoting the words, "The life of a yogi cannot be known by the instances through which it has passed." You'd like to know him. You'd like me to tell you about him—how tall he was, who his mother was, how he wore his hair, the fashion statement of his clothing, where he went to school, where he grew up, how they treated him on the playground. But the closest we can come to knowing an enlightened sage is by transcending and experiencing the universe in our own consciousness. Speaking of instances puts boundaries on the infinite, and then it is not infinite anymore.

Still, we can look at his achievements. Below is the official picture of him put out by the TM® movement.

Since his performance was grand and substantial, we can conclude that he probably could lay to rest a completely small thing like the unhappy chatter in a mind.

What's my own story about him? It's this: He completely changed the direction of my life. I thought I had it figured out. In 1972 I became a Founding Professor at his Maharishi International University, and after two years there in my dream position, he gave me a little advice. "Write a book," he said. I clung a little to my security as an academic, but I became a writer. I collected rejection slips. I read *The Writer Magazine*

Maharishi Mahesh Yogi
Founder of the Transcendental Meditation® program

and read all the current books of advice to young writers until I was fed up. And finally I published something.

To me, his turning me from scholar to writer was a master stroke. He reset my world and left me as what I should be—a writer and a teacher of an ancient anxiety-relieving technique.

A Unique Technique

He did a lot. He was an outpouring of creativity—not just from dawn to dark every day but all day every day, and most if not all of the nighttime, for all of the 61 years he was teaching the TM® program on our planet.

He also wrote some books. They're strong. They're words with a great deal of organizing power. I read through his first two books in 1970 when I was introduced to the TM® technique. I approached them as if I were reading a usual text of some sort, the way I read them in my PhD studies. Now I can read only a few paragraphs at a time in his works titled *The Science of Being and Art of Living* and *Maharishi Mahesh Yogi on the Bhagavad-Gita: A New Translation and Commentary, Chapters 1–6*. They're too dense for me now. I have to pause and let the insights sink in. He also wrote a bunch of little monographs that also cause one to pause and read closely. The footnotes run longer than the text in these small works. But they are compact, pure impulses of insight into subjects that include government, education, and health viewed in the light of consciousness.

So, okay. First of all, he brought his technique to the world. I should have started there, I guess. Suppose this technique is what I say it is—a technique that anyone can do—a child, a demented person, an ordinary person or a genius. When this or that or the other person does it, he or she begins to transform in the direction I have been explaining. People begin to be comfortable with themselves. Problems diminish.

What else did he do that was worthy of note, besides his passing along the technique and offering it to everyone? Well, he taught it to the Beatles. I have seen a video where one of them, Ringo, I believe, said that they didn't even think he knew who they were although Beatlemania was at its peak. However, his instruction to a few mop-headed boys from England made his technique universally famous, and for several decades of my lifetime it was increasingly rare for anyone not to have heard of the Transcendental Meditation® program. However, much to my surprise, not having heard of TM® has happened a few times recently, and I also encounter a lot of "who's Maharishi?"

I'm not sure he personally originated any of the techniques he taught, such as the basic TM® technique. They came from ancient traditions. But he was the one who passed them on to the rest of us. He developed advanced techniques that enriched and accelerated all the effects of his basic technique. Then he developed his TM®-Sidhi® program including Yogic Flying. He was the first yogi in modern times, I believe, to teach Yogic Flying and, even though lots of imitators claim to do the same thing as his basic technique, they don't generally teach his method of flying. Maharishi was the one who taught what is known as yogic flying and trained administrators who continue to teach it.

According to one former leader of his movement, he trained about 12,000 teachers in his basic technique, of which I'm one. The training takes five months. Only five months. It took me nine years to earn my PhD, and though I love having the higher degree, I can't do nearly as much for anyone with my PhD training as I can by teaching someone the TM® technique. (When I got to graduate school at Northwestern and found that the study of literature was the same as in my undergraduate training at Hamilton College, I speculated leaving the institution and offered to leave my studies. A wise and nurturing dean, Dean Robert Baker, talked me out of it. "You'll be able to raise someone from here to here," he said, with hands low, "but you'll never be able to raise one from here to here," with hands high. I am grateful for his advice. I'm glad I finished. But even when I completed the program, I felt I couldn't raise people high enough and again had the urge to leave my profession.) The PhD is about ideas and theory rather than giving an experience (the transforming experience of transcending) to the students, and I was fairly burned out along the way to earning it. When I teach the TM® technique instead of English literature, I know I am offering an experience to someone.

He Made Sense of Mysticism

Maharishi systematized that abstract state, previously thought of as "mystical," that we grow into as we develop consciousness. Maharishi first identified transcendental consciousness, the state when you experience that inner expanded field by itself. He identified the fifth state, Cosmic Consciousness, when you live in unboundedness all the time when awake, dreaming, and sleeping. We don't usually grow into the state of higher consciousness without transcending, but with regular sessions of transcending, we can grow into it. And some people are born in a higher state or stumble into it. Walt Whitman's biographer said Whitman lived in the state of cosmic consciousness along with Christ and Buddha (heady company, certainly). There can be a lot of confusion about cosmic consciousness, but Maharishi made it systematic and tested it scientifically. You experience it. You display alpha and delta brain waves at the same time during sleep. Viewing consciousness in the light of science, the abstract becomes mechanical and measurable.

After cosmic consciousness, which you would think would be the complete realization of human potential, come two others. The sixth state of consciousness is when the outer world is filled with love and shining with a golden glow. Not too many in the past have ever known they were in it, although certainly artists and music composers and poets have envisaged it. William Blake, the 18th century poet, seemed to experience it. ("Tyger, tyger, burning bright," and so on.) Then, for total realization, comes unity consciousness where the inner is uninterrupted pure consciousness, and the outer is uninterrupted pure consciousness; hence both are one and the same. Life is complete. Maharishi identified the states of consciousness that before him were undefined experiences of mysticism, difficult to define in everyday terms even for those who were having them.

He encouraged, oversaw, and inspired scientific testing and validation of states of consciousness. "We'll test it." Over and over and over. There have been close to 700 studies of the Transcendental Meditation® program so far. Here's a story of this:

A young student at UCLA named Keith Wallace began practicing the TM® technique, became a teacher of the TM® program, and either encouraged by someone, or simply on his own, became fascinated with a single question: "How in the world do you test for something completely unmanifest, the field of pure consciousness inside?" Who knows what trial and error he had to go through to arrive at a method of measuring consciousness, and he was at Harvard working on his PhD when he began to develop his work on this. But in 1970 he tested breathing rate, sweating, and levels of a stress hormone to compare these physical properties during the practice of the TM® technique with properties of a subject who simply had his eyes closed. Dr. Wallace's work started a trend that has become standard. How do you measure consciousness, which is abstract? By measuring the body, which is physical and measurable.

Maharishi's worldwide movement began to take shape, led by a group headed by Dr. Robert Keith Wallace (known as Keith Wallace). Students International Meditation Society (SIMS) swept the nation, catching me in its net, and, I am convinced, ended the trend of the time of students engaging in violent outbursts on campus with building occupations and ugly protests like those at the 1968 Chicago Democratic Convention and later at Kent State where a young coed was killed.

He developed a World Plan for making the TM® technique available to anyone anywhere. Boosted by a worldwide program following his death in 2008, the universal opportunity to learn the liberating practice has increasingly become a reality. Want to learn the TM® technique? You probably can, wherever you are. Tanzania? No problem. Teachers are available. You can learn the TM® technique in Dar Es Salaam. It's all over the place in Nepal. You can learn it in South Korea, from the Lees, whose head actually belongs to the royal family that ruled the country until about 100 years ago. Ecuador? Sure. Haiti? I'm not sure, but it needs it. I know you can learn in neighboring Jamaica. North Korea? I don't think so, but slip into South Korea or Japan and learn.

He Brought Back Ayurveda

He gave a big boost to the ancient health practice, Ayurveda. He explained its basis in consciousness and put it at people's fingertips just like the TM® technique itself. Here's your body type. Here's your imbalance. Here's how to restore order. Here's where your body is messing up (*pragya aparadh*, Sanskrit for "the mistake of the intellect"). Here's how to dive in and fix that, as a supplement to your twice daily practice of the TM® technique.

The longer he went, the more he brought out consciousness-based programs. He brought out Vedic Astrology. Astrology has always had its adherents, but he approached it systematically in the light of his theories of consciousness.

He also revived Gandharva Veda music from the perspective of consciousness. Instead of seeing it as pure entertainment he saw it as a means to strengthen consciousness. It was a systematic method of enriching self-development. Listen at the right time of day, at the right time of year to the appropriate sounds, and you feel yourself melting into the fourth dimension and beyond. Fix your health. Fix your outlook. And, oh, yeah, fix your anxiety.

He developed programs in all areas of society. He was very interested in education, especially consciousness-based education. I remember being fascinated in the sixties by books like *How Children Fail* that we devoured voraciously because we knew something was missing and hoped that this author could reveal it all. What was missing, in Maharishi's view, was the transcendent, and Maharishi developed programs so that children could learn a special walking TM® technique and also learn basic principles that explain their world, such as principles like "rest is the basis of activity."

He developed programs in government, business, and agriculture all in the light of consciousness. As he progressed, he began bringing out more and more Vedic wisdom. As creation expresses itself, he explained, it does so with Sanskrit sounds. Gradually, over a few years, he developed the complete "40 Aspects of the Veda," showing how creation evolved from an initial sound into all expressed sounds. Maharishi assembled groups of pandits and trained them so that they could chant those sounds and achieve certain purposes or simply calm the atmosphere of the world.

And he inspired neuroscientist Dr. Tony Nader to develop the correspondence of each aspect of the Veda (such as Rk Veda and Sama Veda) with corresponding aspects of the human body. The fruit of Dr. Nader's work was the book *Human Physiology: Expression of Veda and the Vedic Literature.*

He Taught "Don't Enter from the South."

Maharishi got very, very into architecture. He suggested that negative influences come in from the South and encouraged people not to enter their own homes or any building through a South entrance. (My neighbor in one recent home I lived in worries me a little. His expansive, palatial house faces South and has a gate at the South. You even go into his parking lot from the South. Let's hope he won't have trouble, since South entrances are inauspicious!) Maharishi systematically developed, with Vedic experts and with Western architects, a system of Sthapatya Veda that means essentially that when you live in a home designed properly according to the principles of Sthapatya Veda you are in effect enjoying the protection of the deepest levels of the cosmos.

He had teams of people all around the globe working on his programs, and he would go from time zone to time zone, wearing people out, telling them to "go and rest" when it got too late, then moving to the next one.

He even developed materials that were basically for future generations (maybe for you) because they were simply too far beyond the present generations but had to be recorded because he was here in human form for a while. He did a talk, for instance, called "The tenfold structure of Brahm" that was so abstract and intricate that when I played it once for a group almost everyone straggled out in frustration one at a time. "Brahm" isn't even sound. It's gaps. Silent, structured gaps between the syllables of the Veda. Tenfold, like the tenfold structure of nature at the deepest level, beyond the three-dimensional level that in itself we have trouble understanding.

One person besides me remained after a while, and she asked if she could please listen to it regularly. I mean she didn't understand it or remember it. You didn't have to listen to it that way. It was more a way of being than a way of listening.

Oh, continuing to cherry-pick achievements of his, I see that he proclaimed the Dawn of Sat Yuga, a time of heaven on Earth, which he said had already begun because of the release of stress from the Earth and the growth of higher consciousness. He held a massive celebration in Holland to commemorate the occasion, which my wife and I attended. He had elephants walking around. He paid for luxury accommodations for everyone (hundreds of us, maybe more) and fed us royally in temporary buildings that were so far beyond tents that it insults the architecture to call them this.

Only one small part of his achievement was to offer a simple technique for fixing anxiety.

CHAPTER 26

FAQs

"If it's so great, why isn't everybody doing it?"
(Question I should have included but didn't.)
Answer: "They hadn't read this book yet."

Being out there on the street teaching the TM® technique the way I am,
I hear the questions I pose here all the time. We so want people to have
this technique. Why do we care? Well, not to overstate it, we can live
with it if you don't start the TM® technique. But we want you to have
something real. Not just relief from your anxiety. That's just the opening act. We want you growing in enlightenment. We want you bursting
with bliss and love. But I'm getting ahead of myself. Let's look at some
of these hard questions people bring us.

Aren't you really in this for yourself?

Not exactly. Sure, we thrive if you thrive. "You look good, I look
good," my hairdresser Isabel puts it. Does that mean she's cutting my
hair for herself? We feel good if we have people around us who are smiling, happy, generous-hearted, not stressed, and all such good things.
We (anybody) feel good if we live in a nice house or in nice clothes or
have a nice car. Why not? But that doesn't mean we don't want it for
you. You are the true motivation.

You see someone suffering, you just want to help. Isn't that some bit
of international law or, even bigger, natural law. Here's a person in front
of you, and she's practically twitching in her anxiety. She blames her ex.
She blames her boss. She's falling sick with illness that is obviously stress-
related, such as headaches or chronic fatigue or fibromyalgia. And you
know that in a single stroke you can transform her.

Sure, I suppose, there is a certain thrill in being the instrument
for such a sudden recovery. It's fun, you can say, to be witness to an

instant, completely unanticipated turnaround. It's gratifying, if a bit uncomfortable and embarrassing, to hear the deepfelt "I can't thank you enough for what you've done for me." But in any real sense we're not doing it for ourself. We're doing it for you. Obviously.

He Would Not Give His Wife the Satisfaction

"I'll do something, but why the TM® technique?"

A woman's husband said that to her recently when he saw her making so much progress with her TM® technique. She loved her meditation with the TM® technique. She began feeling fresher during the day. Hassles at her work (she writes for soap operas) impinged less on her psychology. She was more patient with her teenage daughter and, as far as that goes, a softer, more loving wife for that husband.

He saw all that, but he didn't want to give her the satisfaction of imitating her. He wanted to one up her by getting his meditation from his own source. He wanted to be his own man. He didn't want to lose her respect by being a copycat; he wanted to earn it by being original. Whatever. These psychological reasons are quite, we can say, quite on the surface. It's like, "take this medicine and you'll get rid of your cough." "No, I'll take a swig of Coke. It's quite medicinal, and I like the taste." Fine, but you won't get rid of your cough that way. Is it worth it just for your ego? Learn the technique that works.

"I Want it. But why should I need to pay for It?"

That's the universal, right? That's the law of the marketplace. Get something, and get the best thing you can for the least possible payment. But, ultimately, you do want to get it. If that means paying a fair price, pay it.

Once the lottery somewhere was over $300 million dollars. I asked a group of mostly new meditators how many would take that sum if it meant that they could never have had the TM® technique and never have it again. The silence was pervasive. I spoke up and said I would never take that deal, but people expect that from teacher of the TM® technique, so no one was influenced. Another man spoke up, an advanced meditator (and also a percussionist with Cirque de Soleil, but that has nothing to do with it), and he said of the lottery prize, "That is just a number." He would hold on to the TM® technique.

For me, if I had to make that deal, I wouldn't take it for the most practical of reasons. Were it not for the TM® technique, I probably would have not made it to my present advanced years in life. Health is the obvious reason, but I was so alienated and unhappy and pretty ignorant that I was pretty sure to keep going down dead ends and getting into trouble that the outcome couldn't have been good.

You know what's fascinating, too? You can't make this argument in the short term, that is, on the spot. No one buys into it (to use a figure of speech from finance). The meditation pays for itself, materially, over and over again. If it's prosperity you're seeking, become high performance on the inside. First of all, you will perform better, and better performers make more money. But, too, there is an effect that happens as people begin opening up inside to the ocean of quietness. It uplifts them. In the trade we call it "increase in support of nature," and it means that because you are more in harmony with the laws of nature when you practice TM, you not only become more proficient at achieving what you want. You often get carried into unexpectedly higher levels that were not even what you intended (but better).

How about an example? Okay. One fellow learned the TM® technique mostly so that he would have better experiences in meditation than he was having with his sound bowl and sitting with his back straight. I mentioned Josh before. He had the better experience once he started the TM® technique. He also had an up and down career as a soap opera writer. He'd get into arguments about story, grow frustrated, and quit. After he had been meditating for about five years, a colleague said, "He doesn't quit his jobs anymore." He experiences what was unexpected—larger than what he had in mind.

One last point, and then I'll move on to the next difficult question. In our pursuit of self, we are looking for fulfillment. When we desire something, we think it will make us happy. Get it, and it does make us happy. For a while. You know that. Here's the thing with the TM® technique. It's a direct path to fulfillment. We just gain fulfillment inside with each meditation (which means with each experience of transcending). And then, that little bit of fulfillment inside stays there. The next meditation adds a little bit more, and inside the whole thing accumulates like a big bliss snowball. We get the fruits of business success whether we're doing business on the outside or not and whether we're successful or not (but, of course, as a person practicing the TM® technique we'll be clear and efficient and will be successful). It's better than money. Spring a little lucre to learn this technique, and you are getting the universe forever. Not a bad deal.

"Isn't it a cult?"

What is this? I wonder what I'll say about this. There is this, mmm, paranoia in society about cults. Mostly I don't think it's so pervasive anymore. Yoga is going crazy, and people do goat yoga and hot yoga and cold yoga. The leaders sometimes get in trouble for their sex lives, and still we flock to yoga class without fear of joining a cult (for the most part). Everybody works out, at least where I live in Southern California. You get your designer spandex outfit, your workout shoes from Nike, your stretch bands, whatever. It's not a cult.

Everybody goes to the doctor. (I know. You don't. But everybody does.) You get your flu shot. You bow reverentially (maybe figuratively) to the doc, male or female, and you take the little pink pill that he gives you, and you strap on the blood pressure monitor and report the results. Systematized following of a leader, blind following really. (I had a dentist who insisted I needed a $1,000 "deep cleaning," so I did it, even though to this day I have no idea what she did for that money.) Medicine. Not a cult.

Jim Jones is sort of the paragon of cults. He poisoned the Kool-Aid and made people drink it. Nobody wants to be that trusting, but most people truly aren't. It doesn't mean you shouldn't trust anybody or respect people with charisma or, for that matter, drink the Kool-Aid. Be simple, that's all. Most leaders aren't Jim Jones, and the Kool-Aid is just a fruity drink that's a little too sugary but otherwise not bad.

Certain charismatic figures set up families and have multiple wives, sometimes underage, and exact undo admiration, even worship from their followers. I don't know. Aren't those people generally pretty transparent? You run away when you're old enough.

The TM® technique isn't one of those "families." It's an organization. It has leaders. It's nicely run, and it doesn't pressure people to join or to give money or to engage in any kind of inappropriate behaviors. It has leaders deserving of respect, and it's fine to give it. But all this "cult" kind of thinking is a little silly.

One lady happened to come to an intro lecture on a night when no one else showed up. She felt weird. The center is a nice house in a nice neighborhood, and I guess it reminded her of that cult in Rancho Santa Fe (near San Diego) called Heaven's Gate where people committed suicide thinking they would join up with a comet passing by. So she didn't start the TM® technique. Silly. What can you do? Wait for the next one and continue on.

"Can't I try it before I buy it?"

No. Once you try this particular practice, you have it. You own it forever. You can't gain that state of brain coherence, unique to the TM® technique, without actually doing the real TM® technique. Sometimes people innocently enough come to an intro talk and expect to have a meditation session on the spot. You could do that with guided meditation. Maybe that's what Oprah was able to do to offer meditation to the audience on her show. "Close the eyes. Picture a beautiful place." You can do a guided meditation, sample it, and then buy the app if you want to have the whole package.

The TM® technique is not a guided meditation, in contrast. It is this delicious, unparalleled, unique experience of drinking at life at the source. It's not about words. To taste it, you have to have actual instruction in the whole technique. You also can't have just the first day of instruction, where you begin to transcend, and leave the experience at that. You won't understand what you have, as we've noted elsewhere, so, in a sense, you won't really have it until you've done all the four days of instruction, and then, yes, you have to pay for it. (There is a Satisfaction Guarantee, which I forgot to mention.)

"Isn't it just too good to be true?"

No, it isn't. It is true. I had someone come to a lecture with his sister and leave with that simple remark. "Too good to be true." The sister did learn and was completely satisfied, began dissolving stress immediately, and also moved quickly into higher consciousness and the other benefits of the TM® technique that accrue quickly as we practice.

But, you know, I'm completely sympathetic with that fellow. If we didn't have the mountain of peer-reviewed, controlled scientific research to verify the effects, I'd just say that I don't blame him at all for walking out without learning. We do have the research, of course, but I'm lazy, too, and can quite relate to his unwillingness to wade through it or to trust it even though it is eminently trustworthy.

Here's the thing to me, however. *There has to be this somewhere. Gotta be.* Life can't be this unsolvable riddle that it seems to be as we wander through life trying to solve it. There has to be the solution, the right solution, the means to rid ourselves of all limitations on our life and move with great exhilaration into unrestricted happiness. Everything else does not deliver such complete fulfillment or does not deliver it so fast, certainly not instantly. In looking for the thing that does deliver, we can get discouraged, downright cynical. But, still, it's on us to recognize the real thing when it comes our way. The TM® technique isn't too good to be true. It's just good enough.

I love these questions. They come from the hearts of genuine seekers, often so disappointed for so long from so many directions. What is a little painful, though, is seeing people turn away from learning the practice because their doubt is just so great. I'm not always able to satisfy them with words alone. They need the experience, and sometimes they just won't come in and have it. It's like watching cripples come up to the shore at Lourdes, if Lourdes really did do miracles, and turn away, lean on their crutches, and never get the solution. They should plunge in. If it doesn't work, whatever, but don't get just to the edge and then not get in.

It's a little annoying to see people come, needy people, and never partake. One woman in her forties told me she had a dilated aortic root. I so wanted her to start, not realizing at that time that my own aortic root was dilated and that I had outlived the projections for my life span mostly because I did the TM® technique, and the TM® technique lowers blood pressure. She wouldn't accept my cogent words. Never started the TM® technique as far as I know. That's just the way it is. Can't cry over it. "Raise the voice in the air, and come who comes," Maharishi would say. But, of course, teachers of the TM® technique have a lot of autonomic stability and just smile and carry on, offering the technique to the next taker. What else are you going to do?

Most people who go so far as to come to the introductory lecture do tend to start. I have told you some of the outcomes with people like those in the first chapter who ache and grieve and suffer identity crises and tremble and just hurt. What happens to them when they learn? All those people, I said in the beginning, are a cross section of a stressed society. Their need cries out for expertise. Social workers. Psychologists. Life coaches. PhDs, teams of them, in specialized areas of psychology and medicine and general human behavior. When they come to the TM® technique, amazingly, they get just me or whatever certified teacher of the TM® program is there, someone who has had five months of training that consists largely of time spent with the eyes closed having direct experience of consciousness. What can these seemingly ill-equipped people, the teachers of the TM® technique, possibly do for this diverse group of desperate and hopeless people? Everything. Finally, the solution.

"Don't people sometimes stop meditating?"

People sometimes wonder why they should keep meditating. Nothing is wrong. Such is the issue I've mentioned for the fellow in a previous chapter who lived with his parents and was having trouble getting his business off the ground. His anxiety was now gone. He felt comfortable, natural. But he was still living at home and his client list was the null set. "So," he wondered, oblivious to his lost anxiety, "why should I meditate?" Such is the case with many other persons doing the TM® technique that I have met. "I feel great. I forget that I felt rotten before. So why should I meditate?" Often, too, when they have tried stopping for a while, I hear the promise, "I'll never stop the TM® technique again."

Often I meet these people who are seeking a reason to meditate when they come back to restart. Take Fred. He came back with great

220 E N D A N X I E T Y !

energy and enthusiasm to restart, having had heart bypass surgery
in the interim. "If I'd kept meditating," he once lamented, "I probably wouldn't have needed the surgery." (We've mentioned earlier the
research on the TM® technique and the heart, including research showing lower blood pressure, less weakening of the left ventricular wall,
lowered cholesterol, decrease in atherosclerosis, and less death.) He
might not have. Surely it would have been better to create healthy
cardiac conditions with the TM® technique. I know practitioners of
the TM® technique who have gotten bypass surgery, so he still might
have needed it if he had not stopped meditating. But maybe not. You
like to improve your odds if you can.

The classic, all-time instance of the restart is Clyde, who meditated
for a few years in the eighties, then drifted away from the TM® program.
When he restarted 30 years later, he swore one thing: "Never will I stop
again." He too, of course, laments what he might have become had he
not stopped. But during the lull, he felt fine and couldn't see the need
for transcending.

I don't too often meet the people who stop for good. Why would
they be coming in? But Lois is another one who came back to restart
after laying off for a few years. She had what people sometimes call
"the zeal of the convert," although her conversion was simply her realization of what she had before and should have kept. Often she came
in for group-checking sessions, just to keep herself on track.

Ask people why they stopped, and the answers are invariably
unclear. A common answer is, "I don't know." But where anxiety is
concerned, the answer is much like the one from the working-at-home
fellow mentioned earlier. He wasn't anxious anymore. In his case, he was
still doing the TM® technique. But in many of the cases of those who
stop, the reason is that same one. Think about it. They started practicing
the TM® program for anxiety. Remarkably quickly, sometimes immediately, the anxiety is gone. So. Why continue? They wanted to fix something, and they just fixed it.

It's natural, actually, not to have anxiety. Anxiety is this cruel fric-
tion happening in our psyche for no discernible reason, in spite of our
assigning reasons to it—"What about this meeting next week?" "I'm
afraid to drive." "My career is in jeopardy." All those things are always

in play. We don't have to be tormented about them. And, once the fear is gone, we don't even notice that it's gone. It's like getting a good night's sleep. If you rarely sleep so well, you might feel some gratitude in the morning. But mostly, if it's habitual anyway to sleep well, you don't go around all day thanking God for the night's sleep he gave you. Sleep is natural. Feeling good is natural.

And hence we face the complacency conundrum. People become complacent about the wonderful results they are getting. They're happy, maybe blissful. They manage their addictions or escape them completely for the time being. Business is good. Unexpected strokes of good fortune come to them by the mechanics that teachers of the TM® technique might understand but they may not. (Transcend, and we become attuned to the larger forces of the universe, which carry us to unexpected heights. It's called "support of nature.") All those good things happen. They're all natural. We merge with them, surf in them, all smiles . . . and we forget to do the practice that attunes us to those forces of nature and therefore fall out of such harmony with the grand forces at work at the deeper levels.

Specifically with respect to anxiety, skipping the meditation is like skipping your SSRI. As psychiatrist Norman Rosenthal once said in answer to a public question from me, "It [the anxiety] will come back" if we don't continue to tune in to that quiet coherence that causes that surface disturbance to calm down. We forget. This is human enough. Simple enough. And the forgetting is the great, big risk for all those who turn to the TM® technique to treat their anxiety.

When they start feeling good and enjoying life, they can get so swept up in the pleasure all around them that they forget to enliven the basis of all those good things. It's not a theoretical basis. It's concrete. The laws of nature are inside waiting each day for us to slide into them for a few minutes. No slide, no benefit. Eventually, if we don't take those dives, our negligence catches up to us.

What do we do to try to entice people to continue? I suppose you could ask, "Why do we even bother?" It's very important to the teachers of the TM® technique that our people continue the program. Suppose you give someone a gift, some extravagant, luxury and unlikely gift like a new Tesla (because the results of the TM® technique are extravagant, exceptional, and unlikely, much more than having a Tesla). What is the reward to you for the gift? It's having them drive the car. They don't even have to love it. You don't expect them to appreciate it for long. But there is something very important about having them try it out.

With the TM® technique that has so many benefits flooding in—beginning of course with the decline or ending of anxiety—our students who continue accrue many improvements in life. It's a thrill, like planting a seed one year and coming back in ten years to see a glorious spruce tree where you planted the seed. Teachers of the TM® technique cannot get enough of that thrill, even from students they never see. Somehow, some good karma gathers around the teacher just as it gathers around the student . . . the student who continues, that is.

So we look to inspire students with stories of the glories that follow from regular practice. "Bliss." "Cosmic consciousness." "Support of nature." "Serendipity." "Long life." "Youthfulness." "World peace." "Self-realization." "Feeling at home in the universe." "Immortality (or strides in that direction)."

We do our best, but the conundrum resides in a simple logic. The person came for help with anxiety. The anxiety is gone. They therefore have accomplished what they came for. Unless they realize that the anxiety can return without the regular practice of the TM® technique, and the experience is that they often do not realize such a consequence, then they stop.

We've done our best. We've taught them the practice that brings the relief. Despite their doubts, it works right away, as well for them as for the most advanced meditator using the TM® technique (at least during the practice itself). They asked for a silver bullet for the anxiety, and they got it. The anxiety is dead.

Change is inevitable. Challenges come. We can manage them with aplomb, unaffected, as we do when we are regular in our practice of the TM® technique, and we manage them with increasing calmness and composure as we are regular over time. Yet, horrifying as it is even to contemplate, the anxiety can come back, little by little. Who would ever want that? It's such a simple thing to be regular in your practice of this surprising technique that enlivens the default mode network and neutralizes stress while increasing our energy. Be regular in practicing the TM® technique. Sure, the complacency conundrum awaits. But we don't need to step into it, or at least not for long.

Notes for Figure References That Do Not Appear Within the Charts

Figure 7.4 American Heart Association statement on the TM˚ technique and blood pressure. Figure taken from standard Maharishi Foundation USA materials.

Brook, R. D., Appel, L. J., Rubenfire, M., et al. (2013), "Beyond Medications and Diet: Alternative Approaches to Lowering Blood Pressure": A Scientific Statement from the American Heart Association in *Hypertension: Journal of the American Heart Association* (61).

And on behalf of the American Heart Association Professional Education Committee of the Council for High Blood Pressure Research, Council on Cardiovascular and Stroke Nursing, Council on Epidemiology and Prevention, and Council on Nutrition, Physical Activity and Metabolism.

Originally published 22 Apr 2013.
https://doi.org/10.1161/HYP.0b013e318293645fHypertension. 2013; 61:1360–1383

Figure 9.1 The TM® technique lowers PTSD as well as the gold-standard psychiatric approach.

Reference: Neidich, S., Mills., P., Rainforth, M., Heppner, P., Schneider, R., Salerno, J., Gaylord-King, C., Rutledge, T. "Non-Trauma-Focused Meditation Compared to Exposure Therapy in Veterans with Post-Traumatic Stress Disorder: A Randomized Controlled Trial." *The Lancet Psychiatry*, online version, Nov. 15, 2018.

Figure 10.2 There is a dramatic drop in anxiety for those doing the TM® technique.

Reference: Orme-Johnson, D. W., and V. A. Barnes. 2013. "Effects of the Transcendental Meditation Technique on Trait Anxiety: A Meta-Analysis of Randomized Controlled Trials." *Journal of Alternative and Complementary Medicine* 19, 1–12.

Figure 10.3 Calmer in the daytime, calmer in the nighttime, calmer all day long

Reference: Walton, K.G., Pugh, N., Gelderloos, P., & Macrae, P. (1995). Stress reduction and preventing hypertension: Preliminary support for a Psychoneuroendocrine Mechanism. *Journal of Alternative and Complementary Medicine*, 1(3), 263-283.

Figure 13.1 Brain-Wave Coherence

1. Here is the list of references for data shown in the labels in chart 13.1:

Correlation of EEG coherence with cognitive and affective variables, with reference.

More frequent experiences of TC, p = .05 [1]
Greater Self-Awareness, p = .01 [2]
Increased Inner Orientation p = .004 [3]
Improved Neurological Efficiency, p = .02 [1]
Increased Moral Reasoning, p = .005 [3]
Increased Creativity, p = .001 [4]
Increased Intelligence, p = .005
Improved Concept Learning, p = .05 [6]
Improved Grade Point Average, p = .005 [5]
Increased Emotional Stability, p = .001 [3]
Decreased Trait Anxiety, p = .003 [3]
Decreased State Anxiety (p .005) [3]
Degreased Neuroticism (p = .012) [5]

References for Participating Scientists for Data in Figure 13.1

1. C.T. Haynes, Hebert, R., Reber, W., Orme-Johnson, D.W. "The Psychophysiology of Advanced Participants in the Transcendental Meditation Program: Correlations of EEG Coherence, Creativity, H-reflex Recovery, and Experiences of Transcendental Consciousness." In *Scientific Research on the Transcendental Meditation Program: Collected Papers, Volume I*, edited by Orme-Johnson. D.W., Farrow, J.T., 208–212. Livingston Manor, NY: Maharishi European Research University Press, 1976.

2. D.W. Orme-Johnson, Clements, G., Haynes C.T., Badawi, K. "Higher states of Consciousness: EEG Coherence, Creativity, and Experiences of the Sidhis." In *Scientific Research on the Transcendental Meditation Program: Collected Papers (Vol. 1)*, edited by Orme-Johnson, D.W., and Farrow, J. Rheinweiler, Germany: MERU Press, 1977.

3. F.T. Travis, Arenander, A. "Cross-sectional and Longitudinal Study of Effects of Transcendental Meditation Practice on Interhemispheric Frontal Asymmetry and Frontal Coherence." *International Journal of Neuroscience* 116, no. 12 (2006): 1519–1538.

4. D.W. Orme-Johnson, Haynes, C.T. "EEG Phase Coherence, Pure Consciousness, Creativity and TM-Sidhi Experiences." *International Journal of Neuroscience* 13 (1981): 211–217.

5. D.W. Orme-Johnson, Wallace, R.K., Dillbeck, M.C., et al. "Improved Functional Organization of the Brain Through the Maharishi Technology of the Unified Field As Indicated by Changes in EEG Coherence and Its Cognitive Correlates." In *Scientific research on Maharishi's Transcendental Meditation and TM-Sidhi Program: Collected Papers,* edited by Chalmers, R.A., Clements, G., Schenkluhn, H., Weinless, M., 2245–2266. Vlodrop, The Netherlands: Maharishi Vedic University Press, 1989.

6. M.C. Dillbeck, Orme-Johnson, D.W., Wallace, R.K. "Frontal EEG Coherence, H-reflex Recovery, Concept Learning, and the TM-Sidhi Program." *International Journal of Neuroscience* 15, no. 3 (1981): 151–157.

Figure 13.2 The TM® technique strengthens our immune system.
The specific details of the study showed that those who do the TM® technique have more of the following:

T cells (CD3 + CD4 − CD8 + lymphocytes) that destroy virally infected cells and tumor cells;

B lymphocytes, which identify and neutralize foreign objects, such as bacteria and viruses;

Natural killer cells, which provide rapid response to virally infected cells and tumor formation.

Reference: From the study by Infante, Jose R., Fernando, Peran, Juan I. Rayo, Justo Serrano, Maria L. Dominguez, Lucia Garcia, Carmen Duran, and Ana Roldan. *"Levels of Immune Cells in Transcendental Meditation Practitioners."* International Journal of Yoga 7, no. 2 (2014): 147–51.

Figure 13.4 Reduced Risk of Atherosclerosis
Reference: Walton, K.G., B. Olshansky, E. Helene, and R.H. Schneider. "Trials of Maharishi AyurVeda for Cardiovascular Disease: A Pooled Analysis of Outcome Studies with Carotid Intima-Media Thickness." *Journal of Preventive Cardiology* 4, no. 1 (2014): 615–23.

Figure 16.1 The TM® technique, the great chill-out practice, helps us stay calm in the midst of activity that is normally thought of as stressful.
Reference: Dillbeck, M.C., Orme-Johnson, D.W. "Physiological Differences Between Transcendental Meditation and Rest." *American Psychologist* 42, no. 9: 879-881.

Figure 16.2 Calmer Style of Physiological Functioning: Less Stress in Daily Activity
Reference: Based on the work of Fred Travis and Harold Harung and expressed in their book *World-Class Brain*.

2014 saw three more publications on the Travis Brain Integration Scale (BIS) (Charles, Travis, and Smith 2014; Travis and Lagrosen 2014; Boes et al. 2014). The BIS is a scale created to distinguish classical experiences of higher states of consciousness. (Travis et al. 2002) Previous research has found that the TM program increases scores on the BIS (Travis et al. 2009), and that high scores are characteristic of highly successful people in different professions, such as top level managers, (Harung et al. 2009) world-class athletes, (Harung et al. 2011) and professional musicians. (Travis, Harung, and Lagrosen 2011) Research this year extended this work to show that the BIS, along with other factors, is correlated with flexibility and originality of creative thinking on standard tests (Travis and Lagrosen2014), higher inner development in world class athletes (Boes et al. 2014), and that high BIS scores are also characteristic of successful police officers who possess a spiritual orientation that buffers them against the toxic effects of the stresses encountered in police work. (Charles, Travis, and Smith 2014).

Figure 19.2 The virtuous cycle. How the TM® technique reduces and prevents drug use.
Reference: 1. Walton, K.G., Levitsky, D. "A Neuroendocrine Mechanism for the Reduction of Drug Use and Addictions by Transcendental Meditation." *Alcoholism Treatment Quarterly* 11 (1994): 89–117.

Figure 20.3 Older people who do the TM® technique live longer than those who do not.
Reference: Schneider, R.H., Alexander, C.N., Staggers, F., Rainforth, M., Salerno, J.W., Nidich, S.I., et.al. "Long-Term Effects of Stress Reduction on Mortality in Persons >55 Years of Age with Systemic Hypertension," *American Journal of Cardiology* 95 (2005): 1060–1074.

Figure 20.4 Those doing the TM® technique outlive people who rely on other practices

Reference: Alexander, C.N., Langer, E.J., Newman, R.I., Chandler, H.M., and Davies, J.L. (1989). "Transcendental Meditation, Mindfulness, and Longevity: An Experimental Study with the Elderly." *Journal of Personality and Social Psychology* 57, no. 6: 950–964.

Figure 20.5 Oldsters doing the TM® technique don't feel so old.

Reference: Alexander, C.N., Langer, E.J., Newman, R.I., Chandler, H.M., and Davies, J.L. (1989). "Transcendental Meditation, Mindfulness, and Longevity: An Experimental Study with the Elderly." *Journal of Personality and Social Psychology*, 57, no. 6: 950–964.

Figure 20.7 The TM® technique helps keep telomeres long for longer.

Reference: Shanthi Duraimani, Schneider, Robert H., Randall, O.S., Nidich, S.I., Xu, S., Ketete, M, . . . Fagan, John (2015, Nov 16). "Effects of Lifestyle Modification on Telomerase Gene Expression in Hypertensive Patients: A Pilot Trial of Stress Reduction and Health Education Programs in African Americans." PLoS ONE, 10(11), e0142689. doi:10.1371/journal.pone.0142689.

Acknowledgments

When I first started writing books, I used to wonder how the authors could have so many people to thank. Writing is so solitary. Well, I've learned. Writing is one thing. Publishing? Different story. Indebtedness accrues by the day.

My first and foremost "thank you" is clear and unmistakable. Kenzi Sugihara, Founder, President, and brain trust of publisher SelectBooks in New York. This is my third book with Kenzi and the first when I am the sole author. I have always dreamed of the status in life where publishers bid against each other for my books, clambering to satisfy a loyal audience of readers. Thirty some books later I am still waiting for the bidding war. Perhaps this time. But Kenzi at least does seek me out, knows me, knows my work over a couple of decades, and values the work and the opportunity it brings.

But here is the big contribution from "Dr." Sugihara, as I affectionately call him. When I was writing this book about a specific technique of Transcendental Meditation® offered by a specific organization, he called upon me to approach the organization, *my* organization, where I have worked over a lifetime, and seek its approval for the manuscript soon to be published. Winning their acceptance and support makes all the difference, not just for the book but for its author (who prefers being an "approved author" to whatever name we give for the other type). Thank you to Sam Katz, who recently moved on from being head of communications for Maharishi Foundation USA, and granted this approval (while, of course, issuing a couple of parting cautions as well).

With approval in hand, the other acknowledgments seem to increase exponentially. Before listing them, though, I thank my literary agent, William Gladstone of Waterside Productions in California. Friend for decades. Thank you, Bill, for the introduction to Kenzi 25 years ago and for the recommendation to go with him this time as well.

While I am acknowledging Californians, thank you to Michael Love of The Beach Boys, a rock and roll legend and longtime friend, for lending lightness, credibility, and fun, fun, fun to the book by contributing his Introduction.

Next to thank are the scientists upon whose work on this otherwise too-good-to-be-true technique the book depends to establish its believability. Dr. John Hagelin, thank you so much for permitting the use of essentially all the charts that appear in the book, most of which are the property of the TM® organization and in many cases developed by none other than yourself.

The second scientist I wish to thank, who should just as well be first, is the endlessly dedicated Dr. David Orme-Johnson, who is a living, breathing encyclopedia of information about scientific research on the Transcendental Meditation® Program and the originator of no small amount of it himself. Eager to share, he has been sending me up-to-date PowerPoints and news releases for many years.

I extend my great gratitude to Dr. Robert Keith Wallace, who graces the beginning of this book with a foreword. A prolific author himself, Dr. Wallace was Founding President of Maharishi International University, and earned that position in no small part from his research so pivotal that words like "seminal" and "groundbreaking," even "iconic" fail to capture its value. His work for the first time quantified nothing less than unmanifest consciousness itself.

I wish to also acknowledge all the other scientists whose work on TM® appear in these pages. Dr. Fred Travis studies brain waves as if he looks inside the brain. Forget the "as if." He boldly does the comparisons with Mindfulness he once explained to me just had to be done. No subjective report is up to the task of comparing two different sets of experiences inside the brain. Dr. Travis measures brain activity and makes evidence-based comparisons.

Side by side with him in a key study is Dr. Jonathan Shear. To Dr. Sanford Nidich I say, "Thank you, sir." My inquiry seeking his approval brought an immediate, one-word reply: "Yes." His name appears on many studies, but for me the most important was a Veterans-Administration-funded study showing that TM® was as effective against PTSD as the gold-standard psychiatric approach in the field.

Dr. Robert Schneider is a definer, simplifier, and relentless pursuer of incontrovertible evidence. He has won millions in grants from the American Heart Association and has done studies that simply leave no doubt as to the deep and lasting benefits of TM® for the cardiovascular system. Now he has turned his scrutiny to the TM® program and aging and is doing groundbreaking research on telomeres.

David Shapiro is a rescuer of refugees and a researcher on the results. He has demonstrated the effects of the TM® program for trauma that I use to illustrate just how fast, complete, and unlikely the results from TM® can be under even the worst of conditions. Dr. Kenneth Walton performs with the range of an artist and the persistence of the researcher. His work on addiction as on many other subjects is invaluable, casting light on the chemicals in our bodies. He and Dr. John Fagan are among those establishing that the TM® program affects gene expression. Dr. Charles Alexander's legacy remains huge with his studies on addiction and aging and much more. Thanks, too, to Dr. Maxwell Rainforth, skilled statistician. Dr. Robert E. Herron, from the side of business, demonstrates the effects of the TM® program on the bottom line of a company.

In another vein, I want to acknowledge all the teachers of the Transcendental Meditation® program, worldwide legions of what I think of as "catchers in the rye." I can write a book like this, where we recommend that people learn the technique feet-on-the-ground with a live teacher, only because there is a network of teachers all over the Globe and, especially, all over the US.

Here is a nod, too, to the need of mankind that brings us to create such a book as *End Anxiety!* in the first place.

I am completely indebted to all the TM® meditators whose stories appear in the book and are, indeed, the life of the book. These are real people. The quotations are real. In some instances, with their permission, I use real names. Mostly, though, I use fictional names but always for real people. My inspiration as well as my anecdotes come from daily encounters with people seeking, sometimes desperately, to be happy.

Thanks to my wife, Nina, who wisely refuses to read the manuscript as it is in preparation but nevertheless structures my life so that I am able to prepare it and remain nourished, healthy, and happy. A beloved teacher of the Transcendental Meditation® program, she keeps a stream of candidates and meditators coming through the door (on Zoom a lot these days) and furnishes me with fresh inspiration daily and reinforcement for my own experience that this technique changes lives. Once the book appears, she plans to read it and share it far and wide.

I want to acknowledge the artists who make the book truly professional and even dazzling. Here is one place where the difference between writing and publishing shows up clearly. Professional artists like Janice Benight make the surface look professional and, according to inviolable laws of nature, therefore the content has to be professional as well—no exceptions.

Which brings up, like a bookend to my first acknowledgments to publisher Kenzi Sugihara, the name of his dedicated wife and my editor, Nancy Sugihara. Insistent. Persistent. Vigilant. Neither she nor I like to proofread, yet she forges ahead, always examining for accuracy, truth, and even simple common sense. She reads and rereads and rereads and questions anything even slightly loose or suspicious, leaving no shortcuts for this author who otherwise rather likes the easy way out.

Challenged and revised, I emerge from the editor's readings with a manuscript with as few loose or careless expressions as possible. Nevertheless, any misstatements or errors of any sort are mine and no one else's. I take full responsibility for them.

I would be remiss if I didn't thank Maharishi Mahesh Yogi, who brought this ultimate anti-anxiety technique to the world, even if he did bring it as a method for reaching higher consciousness. Thank you to his successor, now in charge of the worldwide movement, Dr. Tony Nader.

Testimonials from TM® Practitioners

After producing over 600 *Star Trek* episodes and 4 motion pictures, I guess I'm pretty familiar with stress and anxiety. What made me stick around and follow through [with the instruction in the TM® technique], was not only my fascination and attraction to the principles of TM®. It was equally a result of the remarkably warm, patient, and informative leadership of Jim and Nina Meade.

—**Rick Berman**, *Star Trek* Producer

I came to Jim to guide me into the world of TM®, knowing nothing about it. He gently explained to me the goals, the concept, the ease. My time with Jim led me to a more spiritually significant life, with TM® at the core of my journey.

—**Lou Simon**, VP, Music Programming, Sirius XM Radio

Working with Jim was not only an eye-opening experience—it was completely transformative. The act of Transcendental Meditation as it was described to me years before I began was intimidating to say the least; then I found Jim and Nina. Jim walked me through each step slowly, without judgement and with complete ease. I am excited that he is out in the world teaching people of all ages to practice this technique. We are the lucky ones.

—**Marielle Scott**, actor in *Lady Bird, You, A Teacher*

Jim Meade's inspirational talks and books keep me motivated, on track, and in alignment with who I know myself to be. Read this book!

—**Katie Love**, Writer/Producer/Comedian, WriteLaughLove.com (Meade student) *perfectionist x anxiety = disaster*

I was so mad when I started TM®. I felt like a 50-ton whale with so many barnacles on me that I couldn't swim anymore. From the moment I met Jim Meade, his knowledge, joy of teaching, and slightly left of center sense of humor started to knock them off. Early on, he mentioned the word "effortless" and I thought "yeah, right . . ." Now, after several years of his unique brand of "Jimspiration." I can't imagine a day without my two pillars of TM®. I am on track and at peace with my purpose in life. To make people laugh with my heart. Effortlessly. Yeah, right.

—**Clay Bravo**, actress, writer, humorista

Since meeting with Jim and learning TM® I feel a reduction of stress and anxiety, which is saying a lot in this time of the COVID-19 scare. I have done many meditations, and I feel that TM® really reaches the essence of what meditation is.

—**Paul Vargas**, keyboarder for the popular eighties band Missing Persons

Jim Meade should have been one of those writers who got rich writing. But alas. At least he can write—very well.

—**Robert Sanny**, independent publisher

The strange thing is, I went into TM® looking for a fix to a confidence problem—and I got so much more in return. Emotional and psychological stuff that hadn't moved in years moved literally after my first 20-minute session.

—**Ron Cabreros**, Business Exec.

Jim Meade's ability to write is both uplifting and inspiring. Have you read any of his books yet?! I can't wait to read his next book on anxiety since this is the season in which we each are living with it daily!!

—**Lesleigh J. Tolin, M.S.** Counseling Psychology
Certified Advanced Grief Recovery Specialist®

I learned TM® with Jim and Nina. My biggest problem in life is being ADHD. I find myself all over the place throughout the day, never finding a calm moment. That 20 minutes of meditation is the greatest 20 minutes of the day for my head. It's my time to relax. I can do it almost anywhere. I find that calm space and when it's over, I feel more focused. I'm almost 60 years old; my biggest regret was not trying TM® earlier in my life. I'm loving it.

—**Denny Tedesco**, Director of the Wrecking Crew Documentary

Jim Meade has a gift for bringing out the essence of what we need to know . . . before anyone else has done it. He was the first to envision a simple, easy way for the world to understand the revolutionary Voicemail concept being introduced in the mid 1980s: "Voicemail—Use it while you're in, not out!" became the Voicemail Industry's story line and a key element in the proliferation of Voicemail services worldwide!

—**Paul Finnigan**, President, International Voicemail Association

Dear Jim and Nina,

This is to again express my appreciation for your leadership in the Encino Center for TM®, and especially for the synchronized daily meditations, which have added a key ingredient to my life that had been missing for many years. Since "getting with the program" for the past few weeks, I have been enjoying a marked improvement in creativity, mental clarity (especially memory and sequential planning), enhanced sensory perception and overall enjoyment of life. In particular, I notice that I get much less frustrated with irritations and screw-ups, including all matters pertaining to the current pandemic. I also find that a deeper dimension of gratitude and tenderness has developed in my feelings, especially towards my wife and other dear people in my life.

Sincerely,

John Mears

I have lived my entire life with clinical depression inherited genetically from my father's side of the family. That, along with ADD, Childhood PTSD, and Dyslexia thrown in for good measure, is what I brought to my first meeting with Jim and Nina Meade. In spite of working in a high-stress environment 12 to 16 hours a day, the TM® program taught to me by Jim and Nina has been nothing short of life changing. I admit to being a bit reluctant at first to follow Jim and Nina's protocol, but I am so glad I did. Nina's technical explanations, in concert with Jim's thoughtful and entertaining lectures following the weekly group meditations have been a source of comfort and inspiration. By the time I was 3½ years into my journey with TM®, I turned to my wife one evening and gently told her "I am not depressed anymore!" I had been gradually feeling better for some time, and even getting a sense of humor back, but I was afraid to feel as though I could count on it as it seemed too good to be true. I am still practicing and still feeling improvement.

I feel as though TM® has accelerated the psychotherapy I have received (which I believe in and am grateful for) by 10 years. Prior to TM® I had tried many forms of meditation, but I suppose, in part due to my ADD none of them proved effective. If you are suffering (as I was) with depression please consider TM® as part of your therapy. For me it has turned out to be the mainstay of my therapy, and I must note that I do not take any depression medications. I would like to thank Jim and Nina for being such wonderful guides.

Sincerely,
—Joseph Geisinger, Cinema Audio Society member since 1980
Nominated for Oscar and B.A.F.TA. Awards
Best Sound Mixing Motion Picture

Since the 60s and 70s, I have been aware of the Maharishi and Transcendental Meditation®. More recently, I came to wonder what I had been missing. Learning TM® from Jim at my local center was one of the great things I've ever done. A real 'aha!' moment. Negativity, worry, and stress dissolve with the daily practice. Life gets better. Jim said it would be like this!

—Ralph Davis, Software Consultant

Hi Jim,

No, you didn't share the news about the publisher. Congrats—that's fantastic!

My apologies for the delay—I've been having some frustrations with my practice of TM recently (still haven't missed a session though) and was hoping to correct them prior to providing any kind of testimonial, in the effort for it to be as positive and honest as possible—I'm getting there.

That being said, TM® and the practice have been an absolute game-changer for me and my family—especially according to my wife. She's repeatedly shared that I'm far less anxious when it comes to the little things (i.e., our kids ignoring us when we call their names 10,000x; our kids fighting with one another… basically, our kids being the little-shit by-products of the individuals who created them) and far more present when engaging with her, our family, and others.

Personally, I think TM® has really helped me compartmentalize—in a good way. When I'm writing, I'm not worried about our kids or money or anything other than writing, and when I'm doing other stuff, I'm not worried that I'm not writing—THAT used to be a real issue for me; anxiety-wise.

With regard to your instruction, as I've been told, I had a very unique experience when it came to my introduction to the practice—you and I did four one-on-one sessions (due to the pandemic and the lack of other students), which really allowed you to focus on me, my questions, and my experience when it came to learning the practice. You were patient, communicative, and knew a thing or two about basketball—so, that made it all the easier.

I've been practicing TM® for just over fifteen months now, and when I'm around people who I haven't seen in that same time period (in all likelihood, due to the pandemic), they notice the difference in how I carry myself—it's not carefree and aloof, but it's far more present, focused, and engaged. I share with everyone that it's TM® that's the difference.

—S.

Words are just that, words! . . . sign posts to get to a point and the experience is MUCH GREATER than the words! And yet I yearn to say that I feel love, I have these experiences of heavy heavenly vibrations all over my head, the amazing feeling of the tension being released from behind my eyes and nose air passages, being cloaked in this light of love and I do not want to say words I just want others to experience it for themselves. It is interesting to feel such passion about something so natural, so innocent, so loving. Maharishi is absolutely correct in (humorously) saying you cannot forget the experience of the self, once you dip into this ocean of nothingness you can never forget how refreshing the water is.

—**Jerome Buchanan**, Professional Fighter

James Meade is a superstar author who is at home with a wide range of intellectual themes—from the sacred to the scientific and technological. His mind knows no barriers. What's more, he's an incredibly nice person and the perfect collaborator. Even after knowing him for decades and witnessing his brilliance as a writer, I continue to be amazed at his prowess.

—**Dean Draznin**

Transcendental Meditation has been not only a game-changer but a life changer.

—**Brock Bond**, Professional Baseball Player turned teacher of the TM® program

When I was 26 years old I started to smoke weed, and some other different sources of drugs. I tried many years to run away from my self and from the world. And it did work just fine. Bit by bit my weed usage because extremely high I couldn't do and I didn't do anything without it, even when I was 40 when my daughter was born, I was high.

The numbness of my conscience and feelings brought me to choose wrong relationships over and over in my life, especially with my daughter's mom. We had one of the worst relationships that I ever heard of. And I kept running for the weed can using it more and more. I did not realize how it wasn't a source of calm and escaping any more. For me it became a power to drag me down. With the constant fighting with my ex, the weed helped me to lose my self-esteem and confidence. I constantly tried to avoid eye contact with anyone that I met, even friends and relatives. Now I understand how the weed was a source of anxiety for me. I couldn't maintain my life anymore.

As a last resort I was looking for help and in a mysterious way I heard about TM®.

I contacted San Fernando Valley center in California and the voice of a woman was on the other side of the phone. She told me that her husband will do the course for me if I want to sign in. When I ask for the price, I realized that there is no chance that I can afford it. I told her that I am on disability. I was injured at work and I cannot work for a long time. She gave me a big discount, but it wasn't enough and then she told me that they will divide it into payments that I can afford. I felt that I'm already in the right place because of her effort of trying to help me so much.

After I signed in Jim called me to schedule the first day of the course. I told him that I'm using weed excessively and he right away told me that he doesn't teach TM® for people that use substance. I told him that I'm serious and I need it, this is my last resort in life, and I feel that I'm on a dead end. Like his wife he heard my voice and realized that I'm really asking for help. He then said that he was willing to make an exception for me. "Come on Saturday," he said. The TM® technique will help you get rid of it.

Of course I came high that day, I didn't need anything else for so many years. But like a lightning strike through the first meditation tears start dropping from my eyes. I felt extreme peace and relief that I could never explain in words.

Jim and TM® saved my life. Two days after I had no urge in me to stay high anymore. The meditation gave me this pure joy and calmness that I was looking for all of these years. Suddenly I realized that the weed was an enemy to my life and not a helping hand.

TM® made drugs to be insignificant for me and I stopped cold turkey from doing any substances. Since then I had weed around me from friends and occasions and I never had a little urge of going back to it. All I need is my 20 minutes peaceful time twice a day to fulfill my life.

—T. O.

The terms "stress" and "anxiety" are heard frequently these days, and with good reason. The mental/emotional experience of the two is almost the same. Research now indicates that they overlap in physiological sequalae as well. In this eminently readable book, James Meade presents evidence that the technique of Transcendental Meditation dramatically reduces both stress and anxiety, further confirming the close links between the two and showing how practice of this technique can lead to a happier, healthier life.

—**Kenneth Walton, PhD**
Adjunct Associate Research Professor,
Institute for Natural Medicine and Prevention,
Maharishi International University

Jim Meade brings deep knowledge to the surface for all to understand and enjoy. As a seeker of health and truth, I don't know where I would be without his life-changing advice.

—**Anna Dixon**, Yoga teacher, inventor, Mom

I had the pleasure of being taught by Jim. It was the best introduction to TM I could have hoped for. I have since used it as a tool almost daily, and it has given me a sense of peace and a reprieve from the stresses I face on a daily basis as a director and creative executive.

—**Anthony Pietromonaco**
Commercial Director and CCO Company X Media

Index

A

Adaptive reserves, conservation, 94f
Adderall, usage, 172
Addiction, 153
  hormones, impact, 155–157
  management, 221
  sobriety, 113
  TM technique, usage (benefit),
    158–159
Addictive habits, display, 7
Aging
  process, reversal, 163f
  TM technique, impact, 162–164
Agony, numbing, 186
Alcohol use/alcoholism
  reduction, 154–155
  relief, 117–118, 153–154
Allen, James, 33
Alpha1 coherence, 86
  TM, impact, 87f
Alpha EEG coherence, 50
Alpha relative power, 133
Alpha waves, presence, 175f
American Heart Association (AHA)
  TM/blood pressure, relationship,
    53f
  TM/MBSR recommendations,
    contrast, 52
Amygdala
  reset, TM technique (impact), 109
Amygdala, control, 99
Anger, relief, 117–118
Angina pectoris, risk (reduction), 165
Aniston, Jennifer (TM usage), 151
Ansari, Aziz (TM usage), 151
Antibiotics, ubiquity, 162
Antidepressants

side effects, 60
usage, 55
Anxiety. *See* Trait anxiety
  combatting, 88
  disappearance, 186
  escape, impossibility, 11
  examples, 11–16
  experience, 21
  frenzy, 112–113
  impact, 97f, 108–110
  long-term source, 17
  medications, side effects, 59
  mindfulness, impact, 45–46
  permeation, 146
  presence, 12
  problem, scope, 8
  reduction, 75–77
    TM/mindfulness, comparison,
      49f
    TM technique, impact, 49, 76
  relief, 55, 112–114, 119, 161
  side effects, 7
  solutions, offering, 25–27, 199
  TM program, usage, 220
  treatment, 221
  ubiquity, 9
Anxiety, repair
  arguments, 26–27
  backfiring, 22
  impossibility, 19–20
  precedents, perspective, 21–22
  solutions
    hatred, 20–21
    problems, 22–23
Aortic root, dilation, 218–219
Applications (apps), usage, 37
  failure, 39–40
As a Man Thinketh (Allen), 33

Self-blame, rarity, 191–193
Self-confidence, appearance, 95
Self-development, pursuit, 44
Self-help books, problems, 35
Self-realization, 222
Self-repair feedback loops, 96
Serendipity, 222
Serotonin. *See* Selective Serotonin
    Reuptake Inhibitors
  impact, 56, 182
  increase, 60
  levels, impact, 183
  reduction, results, 156–157
Sex addiction, relief, 117
Shear, Jonathan, 86
Sickness (increase), stress (impact),
    142f
Side effects, 57–60
Sleep, awakeness, 174–177
Sleeplessness, 5, 7–9
Smith-Shamey, Silena, 37
Social conflicts, solving (possibility),
    295
Social ills, 189
Social unrest, problem, 195
Society
  finger-pointing, 190–191
  repair, impossibility (feeling), 189
  stress, easing, 192–193
Solutions, offering, 25–27
Songs of Experience (Blake), 164
Sorrow, 3–5
Stephanopoulos, George (TM usage),
    150
Stern, Howard
  depression, 124–125
  TM usage, 150
Sthapatya Veda (Maharishi
    development), 210
Stress
  blind reduction, 193–195
  causes, 90
  dissolving, 89

elimination, 96, 120
feelings, elimination, 17
hormone
  decrease, TM (impact), 77–79,
      157
  secretion, 93
impact, 92–95, 138, 141
impression, 91
interior location, 192
markers, 46
obliteration, 88
physical characteristic, 91–92,
    96–97, 155
pump, 95–97
reduction, 133f
regulation, 107–108
release, impact, 194–195, 211
relief, 119
side effects, 7
stress-related illness, company
    expenditures (decrease), 141–142
suffering, reality, 90–91
TM, effects, 77f
Stroke (decrease), TM technique
    (impact), 106f, 165
Students International Meditation
    Society (SIMS), 208
Substance use, 157
Suffering, description, 8
Suicide
  contemplation/action, 14, 58, 111
  rate, 68
  risk, 67
    increase, antidepressants
        (usage), 60
  thinking, 217
Supaya, W., 93
"Superstring" life, 183–184

T

T cells, increase, 102
Tedesco, Denny, 89
Telomerase, effects, 169f

About the Author

James G. Meade, PhD, sometimes considers himself to be like Henry David Thoreau's "The Artist of Kouroo," who labored outside of any constraints of time and in the words of the famed transcendentalist philosopher, "made a new system in making a staff." For Meade, now 77, the "staff" is this book.

Distinction is nothing new to him. He received his Ph.D. in English from Northwestern University, graduating, as his dissertation director phrased it, "With Distinguished Commendation." As an undergraduate he was Phi Beta Kapa from "Little Ivy" Hamilton College where he received the coveted Frank H. Ristine Prize Scholarship to the top student in the popular and highly competitive Department of English. He was commended by the famed Woodrow Wilson Foundation and by the Danforth Foundation, eventually attending graduate school on a full, three-year National Defense and Education Act fellowship.

A Founding Professor of Literature at Maharishi International University, he taught full-time at the college for its first two years and in fact taught the very first course there. Inspired by Maharishi Mahesh Yogi, he left academe and began his journey into writing in the mid-1970s, with two years invested in a Transcendental Meditation® book, as yet unpublished. Reluctant to write about anything else, he allowed the exigencies of surviving on the planet to draw him into teaching writing (Harvard, Boston University, Cape Cod Community College, Fisher Junior College, the University of Maryland) and into working as a writer in industry (two years with then thriving but now defunct Digital Equipment Corporation) and then into many years as a business writing consultant with a client list that included Lee Enterprises, Voicemail International, Lotus Development Corporation, and the Society for Human Resource Management.

In 1988 he began assembling books for the emerging computer book industry and, ever the Artist of Kouroo, lived in the world of strict editorial directives, unforgiving formulas, and unyielding deadlines. He wrote the first book on PowerPoint (*Using PowerPoint*, which sold 300,000 copies) and a barrage of computer "bibles" and "user" guides and, on occasion, "For Dummies" books while also pouring out columns and feature stories and Dot-Com contributions culminating in his *The Human Resources Software Handbook* with the august John Wiley Publishing in New York.

Ever focused on his TM® intentions, he co-wrote *The Answer to Cancer* with prominent Ayurvedic experts Dr. Hari Sharma and Dr. Rama Kant Mishra while his wife and his inner voice kept telling him, "Write your own books about TM®." With Dr. Sharma he wrote a breakthrough book on genetics, *Dynamic DNA*.

Meanwhile he put to use his certification as a TM® teacher, together with his wife teaching thousands of people how to meditate while also offering weekly advanced lectures that evolved into chapters in the book he was fashioning. While teaching in many parts of the US, including even Alaska and Hawaii, he focused mainly in Southern California. Overseas he taught in Tanzania, Hungary, Nepal, Hong Kong, S. Korea, and Jamaica, and lectured in Vietnam, Cambodia, Thailand, and (briefly) Myanmar.

All that intense and demanding preparation had a single focus and comes to realization now with this, his artist of Kouroo staff, *End Anxiety! Proven Benefits of the Transcendental Meditation® Program.*